UNDERSTANDING ROMAN CATHOLICISM

A Guide to Papal Teaching for Protestants

UNDERSTANDING ROMAN CATHOLICISM

A Guide to Papal Teaching for Protestants

by

Winthrop S. Hudson

Philadelphia

THE WESTMINSTER PRESS

To
Wilbour E. Saunders

ACKNOWLEDGMENTS

Permission has been graciously granted by the following publishers to use documentary materials from their publications, the specific source being indicated in the Notes: The America Press (70 E. 45th Street, New York 17, N.Y.), for numerous quotations from the *Catholic Mind,* including the reprinting of "The Christian Constitution of States" and three addresses of Pius XII on "Catholic Action," "The Lay Apostolate," and "The Apostolate of the Laity"; Benziger Brothers, Inc. (70 Fifth Avenue, New York 11, N.Y.), for material from *The Great Encyclical Letters of Pope Leo XIII* (1903), ed. and tr. by John Wynne; B. Herder Book Company (15 S. Broadway, St. Louis 2, Mo.), for material from *The Encyclicals of Pius XI* (1927), ed. and tr. by James H. Ryan; Beacon Press, Inc. (25 Beacon Street, Boston 8, Mass.), for Cardinal Manning's translation of "The Dogmatic Constitution of the Church" from *The Vatican Revolution* (1957), by Geddes MacGregor; Harcourt, Brace and Company, Inc. (750 Third Avenue, New York 17, N.Y.), for material from *The Pope Speaks: The Words of Pius XII* (1940); *Current History* (Wolfpit Road, Norwalk, Conn.), for material from the March, 1928, issue. Appreciation must also be expressed to a very good friend, Theodore Louis Trost, librarian of the Colgate-Rochester Divinity School, for his kindness in securing photostats and microfilms of various papal documents and for his helpfulness in locating other materials.

CONTENTS

PREFACE

ECUMENICAL conversation between men of differing religious faith is at best a difficult art. Basic convictions that give meaning to life are involved, and it is not easy to discuss our most cherished beliefs with detachment, urbanity, and mutual respect. Ecumenical conversation becomes even more difficult, however, when particular religious traditions are markedly divergent in their fundamental assumptions, for then the participants in the conversation find themselves operating in such a different realm of discourse that even the words they have in common have different meanings. It is this latter fact which makes so many of the encounters between Protestants and Roman Catholics sterile and unprofitable. They do not understand each other, and consequently, even when a spirit of irenic amiability prevails, they seldom find themselves really speaking to each other. In such a situation, Protestants are usually acutely aware of not being understood, of not having succeeded in making clear their presuppositions and central affirmations; but they are not always equally conscious of the fact that they have a responsibility to understand the central features of Roman Catholicism if the process of talking past each other is to be brought to an end. The purpose of this book is to further this understanding in the conviction that whatever promotes mutual understanding will contribute to a more fruitful conversation.

This book may also serve as a contribution to Protestant self-understanding, for in the process of understanding a different tradition it is inevitable that one will become more conscious of the distinctive aspects of one's own heritage. This is notably true of a Protestant's encounter with Roman Catholicism, for Roman Catholicism as it has developed in response to the Protestant Reformation serves as an excellent foil to highlight the essential character of Protestantism. From Roman Catholicism, Protestants may also learn needed lessons about their own weaknesses. Catholic Action, for example, learned much from a study of what Dixon Ryan Fox called the "Protestant Action" of the nineteenth century — the technique of shaping the culture of a free society; and it is possible that the lessons derived from Protestant experience need now to be relearned from Roman Catholicism.

No effort has been made to provide a full picture of Roman Catholic life and thought, for that would involve a book many times the size of the present volume. Attention has been centered on that which is most distinctive of Roman Catholicism, and the endeavor has been to let the Roman Church speak for itself in its official pronouncements. For this purpose certain basic documents have been selected, to which have been appended briefer selections of comment and explication. One incidental contribution of these brief excerpts, which could be multiplied many times and which are limited only by the requirements of space, is to illustrate how thoroughly and consistently the major documents represent the position of the Roman Church. What may seem a disproportionate amount of space has been given to the writings in which Leo XIII sets forth the political theory of the Roman Catholic Church for the simple reason that it was Leo XIII who elaborated in full detail the basic position of the church at this point. It will be noted by the reader that subsequent papal pronouncements presuppose his teaching, and it will also be observed that his teaching is specifically confirmed by his successors.

With the exception of the First Dogmatic Constitution on the Church of Christ, the captions and subheadings in the reprinted documents and quotations are not part of the text. Capitalization has been altered in some instances to introduce a measure of common usage into documents drawn from many sources over a period of almost a century, and occasionally a comma has been introduced or eliminated for the same reason.

W. S. H.

Colgate-Rochester Divinity School

I

BY WAY OF INTRODUCTION

M<small>Y</small> next-door neighbor is a Protestant; and we live in different worlds," writes Father George H. Tavard. "How can we understand or know each other?" he asks.[1]

It is not easy for Protestants and Roman Catholics to understand and know each other, even when they live as neighbors in close proximity. They do "live in different worlds." The presuppositions of the two faiths are so diverse that for the one to venture into the framework of thought of the other is to enter a strange and bewildering country. As Élie Halévy, the noted French interpreter of nineteenth-century England, observed: "Catholicism and Protestantism represent opposite and mutually exclusive views of church government and Christian dogma, indeed of religion and life as a whole."[2]

Difficult as it may be, it is important that Protestants should understand Roman Catholics and that Roman Catholics should understand Protestants. Until this task is accomplished, there is little hope of dealing constructively with the tensions that exist between them. This book is designed to help Protestants understand the church to which many of their neighbors and friends belong by

15

letting the Roman Church speak for itself in its official
pronouncements.

∵

Many books have been written to explain and interpret
Roman Catholicism, both by Roman Catholics and by non-
Romanists. They are of varying degrees of worth. Some are
excellent and some are distinctly inferior, but none of them
is completely satisfactory. The point at which they are unsatisfactory is not difficult to explain. Protestant interpretations are unsatisfactory because they are always open to
the charge of partisan pleading. Sentiments expressed by
Roman Catholics, on the other hand, are no less free of
partisan concern, and they are always subject to repudia-
tion as representing no more than individual opinion. Not
even the most distinguished of Roman Catholic theologians
are commissioned to speak authoritatively for the Roman
Church. The teaching power of the church resides in the
bishops; and theologians, priests, and laymen may participate in it — or rather, collaborate with the bishops in it —
only by delegation. But even the bishops may exercise
their teaching function only in solidarity with and in subordination to the Roman Pontiff, in whom dwells the fullness of episcopal power. It is, therefore, in the Bishop of
Rome alone that the authoritative voice of the Roman
Church is to be found. He alone is able to speak for the
Roman Church in a manner that demands unqualified
assent.

A book that purports to help people understand Roman
Catholicism quite obviously must present those documents
in which the " official " teaching of the church is to be
found, and the " official " teaching is to be found in the pronouncements of the Roman Pontiff. These pronouncements

may have been made either by virtue of his extraordinary teaching power or by virtue of his ordinary teaching power. The first is when he speaks ex cathedra in defining a matter of faith or morals; and his teaching, in this instance, is infallible, irreformable, and perpetually binding. Pronouncements made by virtue of his ordinary teaching authority, however, are no less " official," although they may be " reformable," i.e., the specific application of Catholic truth to particular situations is subject to modification by a subsequent papal pronouncement. In a particular papal document it is not always clear whether or not the Supreme Pontiff is speaking infallibly, but the distinction between the two types of pronouncements is of little practical significance at any given time, for they are both of binding authority. (A brief discussion of the essential characteristics of ex cathedra pronouncements is given in the Appendix.)

∵

It is not easy for one who is not a Roman Catholic to read papal documents with insight and perception. Words have different meanings and must be read within the context of a whole structure of understanding. A non-Catholic, seeking to understand Roman Catholicism, must perform the difficult feat of shedding his own frame of discourse and read the papal documents in terms of the Roman Catholic understanding of the nature of the Christian revelation, the Christian faith, and the Christian church. He must pause repeatedly to remind himself what is actually being said.

By " religion " Roman Catholic documents frequently mean " the religion which God enjoins, and which certain and most clear marks show to be the only one true religion " [3] — namely, Roman Catholicism. By " liberty " Roman Catholic documents usually mean *true* liberty, which is a liberty for truth but not for error. " Faith " to a Protestant is generally understood as a trusting self-surrender of the whole man to God, while " faith " to a Roman Catholic conveys the notion of intellectual assent to a whole cluster of propositions authoritatively validated. Even the word " democracy " has occasionally been given a specialized definition far removed from its commonly accepted meaning.

It is at the point of one's apprehension of the divine revelation, however, that serious misunderstandings are most apt to occur. Both Protestants and Roman Catholics take their stance on the proposition that God has made himself known in and through Jesus Christ. They both acknowledge that Christ is to be known in the church and in the Bible. But they differ as to the manner in which competing claims to the authority of Christ are to be adjudicated. The Protestant, believing that any existing church may be unfaithful, is always compelled to ask the question, What does the Bible say? The Roman Catholic, believing that his church cannot be unfaithful, always finds his ultimate recourse in the question, What does the Roman Catholic Church say? For the one, the Bible is over the church, judging the church; for the other, the church — the Roman Church — is over the Bible, interpreting the Bible.

Both Protestants and Roman Catholics agree that the apostles, as eyewitnesses to the life, death, and resurrection of Christ, were the authoritative spokesmen in the early church. After the death of the apostles, all manner of novel doctrines and strange aberrations were put forward in the name of Christ. As a consequence, it was clear that the gospel was in danger of being perverted and cor-

rupted and the whole Christian movement threatened
with disintegration.

There were two responses to this situation. One was to
regard the pastors, or bishops, of the various churches as
the authoritative arbiters of Christian truth, and ultimately
apostolic authority was claimed for their office. This was
not an entirely satisfactory solution, for many times the
pastors were guilty of the very aberrations against which
a defense was being sought. The other response was to
appeal to the teachings of the apostles, for they alone as
eyewitnesses to the event were able to provide authoritative testimony to the divine disclosure in Christ. Thus to
provide a dependable check against the introduction of
strange and novel doctrines, the principle was seized upon
of limiting authoritative teaching to those writings which
could be most clearly regarded as being derived from the
apostles. These writings were gathered into what became
the New Testament, because they provided the only re-
liable historical evidence concerning the person and work
of Christ. Thus they constituted the only trustworthy authority for the church and the touchstone by which all that
claimed the authority of Christ must be tested.

Neither alternative was without its difficulties. The
Bible, for example, was susceptible to varying interpretation, and hence an appeal to the Bible contained seeds of
disunity. The Roman Catholic meets this difficulty by
affirming that his church alone is the interpreter of the
Bible; and to prevent diverse interpretations within the
church, he is forced to accept some means by which their
respective claims may be adjudicated. In the pre-Reformation church, a general council was generally recognized as
the final court of appeal for the determination of Christian
truth. For the Roman Catholic, the Council of Trent in the
sixteenth century officially subordinated general councils

to the papacy; and since 1870, by the decree of Pius IX
at the Vatican Council, the Bishop of Rome alone is the
authoritative voice of the Roman Church.

The Protestant believes that the unity of the Roman
Church is purchased at too high a price, for it disregards
the ambiguous character of human existence and too often
purchases unity at the expense of truth. The Protestant is
profoundly aware of the imperfections of human existence
and of his own finiteness, creatureliness, and sin. He does
not believe that any man or group of men can pretend to
know fully the mind of God this side of the restoration of
all things in God's final act of redemption. He knows that
his own apprehensions of divine truth are always partial
and colored by limitations of knowledge, experience, and
self-concern. He knows that he or any other man must
always be ready to acknowledge that he is not God and
that, therefore, he may be wrong. He knows that the testimony of the Christian community is generally more dependable than his own individual apprehensions of Christ
and that, therefore, it must be taken seriously and not
lightly disregarded. But he also knows that God's people
have been unfaithful and that God has spoken to them
from time to time through lone individuals and that, therefore, he must always be ready to listen even to the last and
the least of the brethren. He knows that Christ is the Lord
of the church and that Christ judges the church no less
than the world. He knows, therefore, that his ultimate
dependence can never be on the church, that in the end
he must render an account of his own faithfulness to God,
and that he must do his own believing since it is his own
neck that is at stake. His appeal is always to Scripture — to
the apostolic testimony — for the church can never be
judged by its own voice, and that which is called tradi-

tion, while illuminating and helpful, is too amorphous to provide any stable criteria of the mind and intention of Christ. The ideal of the church as a perfectly realized historical and institutional unity is surrendered as an utopian illusion, the Protestant being convinced that perfect unity is dependent upon the perfect man and that such unity is not to be had prior to the Last Judgment. In the midst of the ambiguities of his present existence, the Protestant insists that the Christian is called to be faithful to Christ according to the light that has been made known to him; he knows that however misled he may be and however corrupt his community may have become, there is always the possibility of recovery and renewal if recourse may be had to the testimony of those who were eyewitnesses to Christ's life, death, and resurrection.

The Roman Catholic escapes the force of this Protestant analysis by responding with the bold affirmation that in the Roman Church the ambiguities of human existence have been fully resolved, that the Roman Church as a divinely established historical institution is free from the possibility of error, that it is able to know and to declare the mind of Christ fully and dogmatically, that in the person of the Roman Pontiff it possesses an unerring teacher of truth who occupies " upon this earth the place of God Almighty " and who can rightfully demand " complete submission and obedience . . . as to God himself." [4] However one may evaluate this claim, one must always keep it in mind when reading documents of the Roman Catholic Church. When Peter's injunction that we must obey God rather than men is cited, the Protestant is inclined to agree. But when he remembers that, for the Roman Catholic, to obey God is to obey the Roman Catholic Church and its Supreme Governor, the Bishop of

Rome, he finds himself compelled to dissent. For he believes that to obey God may sometimes necessitate disobedience to any church.

∵

There is a further difficulty in reading papal documents
with understanding. Roman Catholic theologians rightfully remind us that papal pronouncements must be interpreted within their historical context, in the light of the
specific problems with which they deal and in terms of
the intention of the Pontiff who issued them. The careful
qualifications that are introduced into papal propositions,
it is insisted, must also be observed. This double caution
is well taken and should be heeded, but it is susceptible
to abuse.

The conclusion, derived from these cautions, that only
Roman Catholic theologians are competent to interpret
papal pronouncements may be acceptable to Roman
Catholics, but Protestants cannot abdicate their responsibility to read and to form their own judgment as to what
is being propounded. Roman Catholics are accustomed —
rather, they are directed — to accept the guidance of those
who have been commissioned by the hierarchy to form
their opinions in matters of faith and morals. But Protestants, without the implicit faith of the Roman Catholic,
are not equipped to accept the assurances of a Roman
theologian as to the meaning of a specific papal teaching.
For good or ill, Protestants must read for themselves, use
their own minds in analyzing its meaning, and draw their
own conclusions.

Actually, Protestants may be misled by restive spirits
within the Roman Catholic Church who are seeking to
liberalize the position of the church. In their zeal to stretch

the limits within which they are free to do their own thinking and to adjust papal teaching to contemporary currents
of thought, some of the more liberal Roman theologians
have been tempted to minimize the doctrinal force of
many papal pronouncements and, by ingenious methods
of historical criticism, to explain away the clear teaching
of the Roman Pontiff. This tendency is accentuated in
encounters with Protestants, most notably in informal
conversations. Frequently, a Protestant is given the im-
pression that papal documents are often a species of ecclesiastical double talk, largely devoid of meaning. Other
pronouncements, it is suggested, have no real application
because the Pope was misled and mistaken in his analysis
of a particular situation, and hence his conclusions are
based on assumptions that were subsequently shown to
have no basis in fact.

To one who stands outside the Roman Church, there is a
real element of tragedy here. For, involved in this subtle
casuistry, there is a sincere attempt on the part of many
theologians to carve out for Roman Catholics a larger area
of freedom in which they are at liberty to think and to
come to terms with some of the most pressing problems of
our time. The tragedy is this: as soon as they have gained
some independent standing ground by means of a particular apologetic, the discipline of the church is tightened
and they are forced to fall in line. The most recent disciplinary pronouncement of this sort was in 1950, when theologians were reminded that even those matters taught by
the ordinary teaching authority of the Bishop of Rome demand consent and that when the Roman Pontiff passes
judgment on a subject in dispute, that subject " cannot be
any longer considered a question open to discussion." The
theologians were further reminded that the plain force of

papal teaching must not be evaded by subtlety, for God's purpose in providing "a living teaching authority" is to make plain that which may be obscure or only implicitly contained in the deposit of faith.[5]

∵

It is probably well for the Protestant reader also to re-member that the Roman Church as we know it is a rela-tively modern creation. In the pre-Reformation church there were two contrary tendencies. The one, represented by the papal party, sought to centralize authority in Rome; the other, represented by the advocates of what we may call "home rule," defended either the rights of the bishops in their own dioceses or of the national churches within their own territories. They were all Roman in the sense that those churches today in communion with Canterbury are Anglican, but the notion of any unqualified obedience to Rome was never more than a minority view.

Papal claims to govern the whole church were set forth as early as the fifth century. It is obvious enough that these claims were never made good among the older churches of the East, although this fact is sometimes for-gotten. It is not so generally recognized, however, that the papal party represented little more than a minority posi-tion in the West. The Roman understanding of the faith, to be sure, did emerge triumphant among the barbarians who had been evangelized by the Arians, and the non-Roman Christianity of Ireland — which was such a dy-namic force in the conversion of the peoples of northern Europe — did ultimately conform to Roman practices and usages. But they scarcely regarded this as submission to a Roman obedience.

The two tendencies can be clearly seen in the relationship between Charlemagne and the Roman Bishop, Leo III. When Charlemagne came to the rescue of Leo, defeated the Lombards, and was crowned emperor by the grateful Leo, the two parties interpreted the meaning of the latter act differently. Charlemagne had long regarded it as his inherited duty, confirmed by Leo's act of fealty, to protect but not to obey the Bishop of Rome. His coronation as emperor he interpreted as further confirmation of his status as a Constantine, called of God to rule in both state and church within his domain. Although he zealously pushed reforms designed to bring Frankish Christianity more closely into accord with Roman regulations, he did this for the good of the Frankish church rather than for any theory of papal authority. He felt no hesitancy in summoning councils on his own authority, and on occasion had decisions passed that ran counter to papal instructions. He appointed bishops, defined the boundaries of their dioceses, drafted regulations for the monasteries, and felt competent to settle controversies, restrict pagan customs, and correct the morals of the clergy. Leo's act in crowning Charlemagne, however, was interpreted by succeeding Bishops of Rome to mean that they could make and, if need be, unmake emperors. But Charlemagne would never have granted this premise by which he could be compelled to render obedience to the See of Peter.

Other kings and princes were no less determined to safeguard their own prerogatives and those of their bishops. The height of papal power was reached in the eleventh, twelfth, and thirteenth centuries, but the actual authority exercised by the Bishops of Rome during this period has often been exaggerated. Rulers acquiesced to papal decrees when it was to their advantage to do so, and ignored them when it was not. Thus William the Conqueror was easily persuaded to invade England with the papal blessing when Hildebrand wished to get rid of the archbishop of Canterbury. But, once having seized the English crown for himself, William refused to do homage for it to the Pope, installed his own men as bishops, refused to permit them to make any appeal to Rome without his consent, and would not allow any papal bull or letter to be received in England or any papal legate to be admitted without his approval.

On those occasions when a temporal ruler seemed to knuckle under to the papal will, it was often the result of pressures more compelling than papal displeasure. King John surrendered England to Innocent III and received it back as a fief in a desperate effort to save himself from the consequences of his own folly in alienating all possible support. The gamble, however, was unsuccessful, for he was forced to come to terms with the barons and signed the Magna Charta at Runnymede in 1215. Nor could Innocent help him, even though he declared the Great Charter null and void and excommunicated the barons. Even the emperor Henry IV, who humbled himself before Gregory VII (Hildebrand) at Canossa, was not tamed, and it was Gregory VII who died in exile. On occasion, of course, bargains were struck that were mutually advantageous. But there was always a wide gap between the role that the Bishops of Rome claimed for themselves and the authority that others were willing to acknowledge.

By the end of the fourteenth century, it was clearly apparent that a papal monarchy was utterly incapable of bringing any sort of unity to the church in the West. Since 1378 there had been two Popes, and with the rival Popes excommunicating each other, a scandalous situation had been created. Confronted by this impasse, a notable group of university professors, who recalled the role of the great ecumenical councils in an earlier time, began to advocate the establishment of a representative form of government in the church to heal the schism and to introduce long-needed reforms. As a result of their efforts, the Council of Constance met in 1414, deposed the rival Popes, and installed Martin V in their place as the chief administrative officer of a newly fashioned conciliar government of the church. The constitution that was adopted provided that another council should be held in five years, another in seven years, and one every ten years "forever after." Councils did meet in 1423 and 1433, but the whole program was undermined by Martin V, who repudiated his constitutional obligations and sought to consolidate his own authority in the church by negotiating separate concordats, or bargains, with each of the national rulers. Thus the representative government of the church that had been fashioned at Constance was not able to function, but the superior authority of a general council in the life of the church continued to be generally acknowledged by a Thomas More as well as by a Martin Luther.

While both the Roman Catholic Church and the various churches of classical Protestantism may be said to represent a continuation of the pre-Reformation church, the sixteenth century witnessed such a decisive reordering of church life in both camps as to constitute a new beginning. It is not surprising, therefore, that the Roman Catholicism that emerged from the Reformation should have been called "the new Trent religion." The decisions of the Council of Trent made central and obligatory for one portion of Western Christendom many things that hitherto had been peripheral and permissive, and one of its main endeavors was to make sure that any future council of this portion of the church would be under the control of the papacy. The Bishop of Rome alone, it was affirmed, could summon a council, and its decrees would not be effective until promulgated by him. Thus the Pope was henceforth to possess a veto both over any independent assembling of a council and, once it had been convened, over its decisions. Conciliar authority was not denied, but in terms of its practical significance it was largely emasculated.

Although the Council of Trent circumscribed for the adherents of the new Trent formulations the independent authority of a general council, it did not deal with the old issue of centralized power in the church versus home rule. Indeed, the Roman Church found it necessary, in order to combat the Protestant advance, to concede even greater autonomy to the national churches. In spite of this fact, the decrees of the Council of Trent were accepted by the chief Roman Catholic powers only with qualifications, and in France they were neither officially received nor promulgated. The Roman Catholic princes simply refused to let the papacy control the ecclesiastical policies to be pursued within their domains; and in Venice, when the papacy attempted to impose an interdict, even the clergy refused to observe it.

The classical formulation of the home-rule, or Gallican, principles was drafted by Bishop Bossuet in 1682 on the basis of an earlier declaration by the theological faculty at Paris. The home-rule, or Gallican, position was set forth in four articles, which combined the points of view of both episcopal and royal Gallicanism. The first declared that kings were not subject in temporal matters to any ecclesiastical authority. The second affirmed the superiority of councils to the Pope. The third was analogous to the American " states' rights " doctrine, maintaining that the traditional customs, usages, and canons of local and national churches were not subject to papal legislation. The last denied that papal decisions in matters of faith were infallible without the consent of the church. The papal court protested vigorously against these four articles that the French bishops and Louis XIV had ordered to be taught in all universities and seminaries. A bitter struggle ensued which was finally compromised in an agreement that left both parties free to hold and teach their respective views.

Although neither side was clearly victorious, the home-rule views of Gallicanism were in the ascendancy throughout most of Roman Catholic Europe in the seventeenth and eighteenth centuries. Throughout these two centuries, the ultramontanists, or partisans of centralized papal power, were fighting a continuous rear-guard action in the church and were losing battle after battle. A measure of the decline of papal power was the progressive suppression of its most doughty champions, the Jesuits, in Portugal in 1759, in France in 1764, in Spain in 1767, and culminating in a general dissolution of the order "forever" by Pope Clement XIV in 1773.

The Restoration at the end of the Napoleonic wars in 1814 gave the papal court and its partisans an opportunity to regroup their forces and to attempt again to establish clear-cut papal control in the Roman Catholic Church. The papal territories in central Italy that had been seized by Napoleon were returned; the Jesuit order was re-established; and the papacy benefited among the restored monarchs of Europe as a defender of the old order of princely rule. Although the papacy continued to lose political battles as a rising tide of liberal democratic sentiment transformed the national governments into constitutional monarchies or even republics in which an increasing degree of religious toleration was granted, the forces of ultramontanism rapidly gained strength within the church. Curiously enough, the growing liberalism in the political order contributed greatly to the strength of the papal party in the church. The new spirit of toleration led to a diminishing sense of responsibility for the church by the state and tended in the direction of a progressive separation of church and state. This meant that the bishops could no longer depend upon the governments of the national states to defend their rights and safeguard their prerogatives in the face of papal encroachments.

In 1854, Pius IX seized the initiative for the papacy in the struggle between the two opposing tendencies within the Roman Catholic Church, and in a bold and dramatic act proclaimed — on his own authority and without any council of bishops — the dogma of the Immaculate Conception of Mary. This revolutionary step was a *de facto* claim to infallibility in the definition of dogma, and it served to place those who upheld the traditional constitution of the Roman Church on the defensive. Sixteen years later, the revolution was completed, regularized, and formalized with the promulgation of a new constitution for the Roman Catholic Church at the Vatican Council of 1870. Papal infallibility was proclaimed as dogma; all jurisdiction was centralized in the papal court; and the last vestiges of episcopal aristocracy in the government of the church gave way to an absolute papal monarchy. Thus the place to begin in an endeavor to understand modern Roman Catholicism is not with the pre-Reformation church nor with the Roman Catholic Church as constituted at the Council of Trent. The key date is 1870, and the key document — basic to an understanding of everything else — is the constitution of the church promulgated at the Vatican Council.

II

THE CONSTITUTION OF THE CHURCH

THE distinctive feature of Roman Catholicism is not those rites and doctrines and pious practices which are most conspicuous and around which discussion of Roman Catholicism usually revolves — the virgin and the saints, relics and images, purgatory and masses. "These bywords with the vulgar," Mark Pattison once observed, are but " powerless decorations." One can be an Orthodox Christian or an Anglo-Catholic and accept the entire sacramental system as it is displayed in the Roman Catholic Church. One can believe in purgatory and private confession, use incense and holy water, make the stations of the cross and say one's beads, and still not be a Roman Catholic. One becomes a Roman Catholic by submitting to what is called " the Roman obedience." The " one essential principle " of Roman Catholicism, to use the incisive words of Mark Pattison once again, is " the control of the individual conscience by an authority or law placed without it and exercised over it by men assuming to act in the name of heaven. " [1] Such is the clear teaching of the Constitution of the Roman Church.

By this Constitution issued at the Vatican Council in 1870, the Roman Pontiff is declared to be both the Supreme Teacher and the Supreme Ruler of the Roman Catholic

Church. As the Supreme Teacher, he alone is the authoritative voice of the Roman Catholic Church in all matters relating to faith and morals. It is for him alone to spell out the doctrinal content of Christian tradition, to provide the authentic interpretation of the meaning of Scripture, and to define and interpret both the content and implications of natural law. The fourth chapter, or article, of the Constitution deals with one aspect of this supreme teaching power, setting forth the dogma of papal infallibility. Although this article has always commanded the most attention among non-Roman Catholics, the key article is the third, which concentrates all legislative, executive, and judicial power — in matters of "discipline and government" as well as in matters of "faith and morals" — in the person of the Bishop of Rome alone. He alone is declared to be the judge of everyone; he alone can be judged by no one.

In the third article of the Constitution, conciliarism is ruled out by an explicit condemnation of any appeal from a papal decision to a general council. All notions of home rule in the church, whether of an episcopal or a royal variety, are repudiated with equally explicit censures. Prior to 1870, the nature of the Roman primacy had not been authoritatively defined in a manner accepted by all. There were some who asserted that it was, like that of Canterbury in the Anglican Communion, a primacy of honor only. Others contended that it was more than that, but that it did not include more than a primacy of inspection and direction. The Vatican Constitution settled the question by declaring the papal primacy to be one of full and complete jurisdiction over the Roman Catholic Church.

The jurisdiction of the Roman Pontiff is both " ordinary "

and "immediate." We are informed by *The Catholic Encyclopedia* that "an ordinary jurisdiction is one which is exercised by the holder, not by reason of any delegation, but in virtue of the office which he himself holds." Immediate jurisdiction is when "its possessor stands in direct relation to those with whose oversight he is charged." [2] In the Vatican Constitution, immediate jurisdiction means that the Bishop of Rome has direct authority — authority that cannot be impeded and that need not be channeled through intermediaries — over the whole church, "both pastors and faithful [the clergy and the laity], both individually and collectively." This is in contrast to jurisdiction that must be exercised through a graduated hierarchy of authority. The most familiar illustration of mediated authority is the feudal system in which the king had jurisdiction over subvassals only through the allegiance they owed to their local lord who in turn owed allegiance to the king. Thus, in the feudal system, the supreme authority could deal directly only with those proximate superiors who were immediately under it, and the obedience of lesser subjects could be commanded only by the intervention of their immediate superior. At each level, the subordinate authorities possessed distinct privileges and prerogatives of their own. The limitation imposed on papal authority by local rights, whether of bishops or princes, were the rights that the Vatican Constitution eliminated with its insistence that the papal jurisdiction was immediate.

It is not difficult to see why the dogma of papal infallibility is of much less practical importance than the dogma that concentrates all legislative, executive, and judicial power in the papal office. When speaking ex cathedra, the Roman Pontiff is able to define dogma that is perpetually binding on the consciences of the faithful; but as Supreme Ruler his ordinary teaching demands full assent — an assent that rules out any further discussion and debate. Furthermore, as Supreme Ruler, the Bishop of Rome has full authority to inform the faithful as to their duty as well as to define their faith, to tell them what they must do as well as what they must believe. The possibility that the Pope may speak ex cathedra, to be sure, does serve as a rather intangible extra sanction to his ordinary teaching, but the important element — whether the teaching is infallible or not — is his power to command consent and obedience.

This centralization of the power of jurisdiction in the Roman Pontiff also effected a revolution in terms of the independent power of Holy Orders which was regarded as being conferred by the apostolic succession in which all the bishops supposedly stood. Pius XII was to acknowledge in 1958 that in early centuries there had been free elections of bishops and that these bishops when properly consecrated by other bishops possessed in full the power of Holy Orders. But the Vatican Constitution made even this independent power of the bishops dependent upon the authorization of the Holy See. It is clear, declared Pius XII, that, by virtue of the power of jurisdiction residing in the Petrine succession alone, "it pertains to the one Apostolic See to judge whether a person is fit for the dignity and burden of the episcopate, and that complete freedom in the nomination of bishops is the right of the Roman Pontiff." As a result, an episcopal election and consecration, which in earlier times would have been valid, now became " gravely illicit," " criminal," and " sacrilegious," if performed without " the mandate of the Apostolic See." Thus what might otherwise be regarded as a valid consecration could not longer be so regarded.[3]

Concerning the Constitution as a whole, a Protestant would make certain comments. The whole structure of the government of the Roman Church rests upon two assumptions. The first is that full power to rule and govern the church was conferred by Christ upon the apostle Peter. The second is that this power was transmitted in perpetuity to the Bishops of Rome.

The first assumption is based primarily upon the text: " Thou art Peter, and upon this rock I will build my church. . . . And I will give unto thee the keys of the kingdom of heaven " (Matt. 16:18-19). There are several difficulties in making use of this text for such a purpose. First of all, Peter had just confessed his conviction that Jesus was the Christ, and the majority of church fathers were in agreement that the " rock " upon which the church was established was not Peter but the conviction he had expressed. This conviction, this faith, is the foundation of the church. Secondly, two chapters later, Christ states that the keys of the Kingdom are to be in the possession of all the disciples (ch. 18:18). Thirdly, the Gospels make it clear that pre-eminence among the followers of Christ was not to be after the pattern of the princes of the world who exercise lordship and authority but in terms of humble service; they were not to command but to serve. Fourthly, Peter continued to be notoriously unstable. Indeed, almost within minutes after Peter had confessed that Jesus was the Christ, Jesus found it necessary to rebuke Peter, calling him Satan for not understanding " the things that be of God " (ch. 16:23). Later he denied his Lord three times in the moment of crisis. (Matt. 26:69-74; Mark 14:66-72; Luke 22:54-61; John 18:17, 25-27.) Fifthly, he was supplanted by James as the leader of the Jerusalem community. He was sent out by those at Jerusalem in the same manner as John and Barnabas (Acts 8:14; 11:22), and when an appeal was made to the council at Jerusalem it was James and not Peter who pronounced judgment (ch. 15:19). It was also to James that Paul reported. (Ch. 21:18.) Finally Peter was criticized by Paul as an unreliable disciple. (Gal. 2:11.) This scarcely gives us a picture of Peter as "the Prince of the Apostles," commissioned by Christ to rule and govern his brethren.

Two other texts are also used to support the Petrine primacy among the apostles. One is Christ's command to Peter: "Feed my sheep" (John 21:15-17), but there is no suggestion in the text that Peter alone is to feed the sheep. The other is derived from the incident when Christ was praying that Peter would be enabled to overcome his instability. "And the Lord said, Simon, Simon, behold, Satan hath desired to have you, that he may sift you as wheat: But I have prayed for thee, that thy faith shall fail not: and when thou art converted, strengthen thy brethren." (Luke 22:31-32.) Roman Catholics usually translate it "confirm thy brethren." There is scarcely a positive assurance here that in the future Peter's faith would not fail (actually it did), and once again there is not the slightest hint that Peter alone is to "strengthen" or "confirm" the brethren.

The second assumption, that the power granted to Peter was transmitted to the Bishops of Rome, has no Biblical evidence — indeed, no early evidence of any kind — to support it. If we assume that Peter was given authority over the disciples, there is not the slightest basis for the notion that this power was to be transmitted to anyone else. But there are further difficulties, for this is not a mere matter of personal succession. Two other assumptions are involved. The first is that Peter was the first Bishop of

Rome; and the second is that his authority was conveyed to succeeding Bishops of Rome. However one decides the debated issue as to whether or not Peter was ever at Rome, there certainly is no evidence that he was Bishop of Rome, to say nothing of being the first bishop of the church there. If Peter was in Rome either by the time Paul wrote to the church at Rome or by the time Paul himself arrived in Rome, it seems likely that mention would have been made of the fact. But the central issue does not revolve around the fact either of Peter's being in Rome or his being the bishop of the church at Rome.

The theory of the Petrine succession is not a theory of personal succession, as is true of the theory of apostolic succession. It is a succession in office rather than a succession of persons. The authority is not conveyed from one occupant of the office to another by the laying on of hands, for an interval always occurs between the death of a Bishop of Rome and the election of his successor. Thus the theory assumes that the grant of authority was not to Peter but to his office as Bishop of Rome, but this identification of authority with a particular office is nowhere to be found in any Biblical text.

With these comments in mind, we turn our attention to the —

FIRST DOGMATIC CONSTITUTION ON THE CHURCH OF CHRIST [4]
(Published in the Fourth Session of the Vatican Council,
July 18, 1870)
PIUS, BISHOP, SERVANT OF THE SERVANTS OF GOD,
WITH THE APPROVAL OF THE SACRED COUNCIL,
FOR AN EVERLASTING REMEMBRANCE

The eternal Pastor and Bishop of our souls, in order to continue for all time the life-giving work of his Redemption, determined to build up the holy Church, wherein, as in the house of the living God, all who believe might be united in the bond of one faith and one charity. Wherefore, before he entered into his glory, he prayed unto the Father, not for the Apostles only, but for those also who through their preaching should come to believe in him, that all might be one, even as he the Son and the Father are one. As then he sent the Apostles whom he had chosen to himself from the world, as he himself had been sent by the Father: so he willed that there should ever be pastors and teachers in his Church to the end of the World. And in order that the Episcopate also might be one and undivided, and that by means of a closely united priesthood the multitude of the faithful might be kept secure in the oneness of faith and communion, he set blessed Peter over the rest of the Apostles, and fixed in him the abiding principle of this twofold unity, and its visible foundation, in the strength of which the everlasting temple should arise, and the Church in the firmness of that faith should lift her majestic front to heaven. And seeing that the gates of hell, with daily increase of hatred, are gathering their strength on every side to upheave the foundation laid by God's own hand, and so, if that might be, to overthrow the Church: We, therefore, for the preservation, safekeeping, and increase of the Catholic flock, with the approval of the sacred Council, do judge it necessary to propose to the belief and acceptance of all the faithful, in accordance with the ancient and constant faith of the universal Church, the doctrine touching the institution, perpetuity, and nature of the sacred Apostolic Primacy, in which is found the strength and solidity of the entire Church, and at the same time to proscribe and condemn the contrary errors, so hurtful to the flock of Christ.

CHAPTER I

Of the Institution of the Apostolic Primacy in blessed Peter

We therefore teach and declare that, according to the testimony of the Gospel, the primacy of jurisdiction over the universal Church of God was immediately and directly promised and given to blessed Peter the Apostle by Christ the Lord. For it was to Simon alone, to whom he had already said: "Thou shalt be called Cephas," that the Lord after the confession made by him, saying: "Thou art the Christ, the Son of the living God," addressed these solemn words: "Blessed art thou, Simon Bar-Jona, because flesh and blood have not revealed it to thee, but my Father who is in heaven. And I say to thee that thou art Peter; and upon this rock I will build my Church, and the gates of hell shall not prevail against it. And I will give to thee the keys of the kingdom of heaven. And whatsoever thou shalt bind on earth, it shall be bound also in heaven; and whatsoever thou shalt loose on earth, it shall be loosed also in heaven." And it was upon Simon alone that Jesus after his resurrection bestowed the jurisdiction of chief pastor and ruler over all his fold in the words: "Feed my lambs; feed my sheep." At open variance with this clear doctrine of Holy Scripture, as it has been ever understood by the Catholic Church, are the perverse opinions of those who, while they distort the form of government established by Christ the Lord in his Church, deny that Peter in his single person, preferably to all the other Apostles, whether taken separately or together, was endowed by Christ with a true and proper primacy of jurisdiction; or of those who assert that the same primacy was not bestowed immediately and directly upon blessed Peter himself, but upon the Church, and through the Church on Peter as her minister.

If any one, therefore, shall say that blessed Peter the Apostle was not appointed the Prince of all the Apostles and the visible Head of the whole Church Militant; or that the same directly and immediately received from the same our Lord Jesus Christ a primacy of honour only, and not of true and proper jurisdiction: let him be anathema.

CHAPTER II

On the Perpetuity of the Primacy of blessed Peter in the Roman Pontiff

That which the Prince of Shepherds and the great Shepherd of the sheep, Jesus Christ our Lord, established in the person of the blessed Apostle Peter to secure the perpetual welfare and lasting good of the Church, must, by the same institution, necessarily remain unceasingly in the Church; which, being founded upon the Rock, will stand firm to the end of the world. For none can doubt, and it is known to all ages, that the holy and blessed Peter, the Prince and Chief of the Apostles, the pillar of the faith and foundation of the Catholic Church, received the keys of the kingdom from our Lord Jesus Christ, the Saviour and Redeemer of mankind, and lives, presides, and judges, to this day and always, in his successors the Bishops of the Holy See of Rome, which was founded by him, and consecrated by his blood. Whence, whosoever succeeds to Peter in this See, does by the institution of Christ himself obtain the Primacy of Peter over the whole Church. The disposition made by Incarnate Truth therefore remains, and blessed Peter, abiding through the strength of the Rock in the power that he received, has not abandoned the direction of the Church. Wherefore it has at all times been necessary that every particular Church — that is to say, the faithful throughout the world — should agree with the Roman Church, on account of the greater authority of the princedom which this has received; that all being associated in the unity of that See whence the rights of communion spread to all, might grow together as members of one Head in the compact unity of the body.

If, then, any should deny that it is by the institution of Christ the Lord, or by divine right, that blessed Peter should have a perpetual line of successors in the Primacy over the universal Church, or that the Roman Pontiff is the successor of blessed Peter in this primacy: let him be anathema.

CHAPTER III

On the Power and Nature of the Primacy of the Roman Pontiff

Wherefore, resting on plain testimonies of the Sacred Writings, and adhering to the plain and express decrees both of our predecessors, the Roman Pontiffs, and of the General Councils, We renew the definition of the ecumenical Council of Florence, in virtue of which all the faithful of Christ must believe that the holy Apostolic See and the Roman Pontiff possesses the primacy over the whole world, and that the Roman Pontiff is the successor of blessed Peter, Prince of the Apostles, and is true vicar of Christ, and head of the whole Church, and father and teacher of all Christians; and that full power was given to him in blessed Peter to rule, feed, and govern the universal Church by Jesus Christ our Lord; as is also contained in the acts of the General Councils and in the sacred Canons.

Hence We teach and declare that by the appointment of our Lord the Roman Church possesses a superiority of ordinary power over all other churches, and that this power of jurisdiction of the Roman Pontiff, which is truly episcopal, is immediate; to which all, of whatever rite and dignity, both pastors and faithful, both individually and collectively, are bound, by their duty of hierarchical subordination and true obedience, to submit not only in matters which belong to faith and morals, but also in those that appertain to the discipline and government of the Church throughout the world, so that the Church of Christ may be one flock under one supreme pastor through the preservation of unity both of communion and of profession of the same faith with the Roman Pontiff. This is the teaching of Catholic truth, from which no one can deviate without loss of faith and of salvation.

But so far is this power of the Supreme Pontiff from being any prejudice to the ordinary and immediate power of episcopal jurisdiction, by which Bishops, who have been set by the Holy Ghost to succeed and hold the place of the Apostles, feed and govern, each his own flock, as true pastors, that this their episcopal authority is really asserted, strengthened, and protected by the supreme and universal Pastor; in accordance with the words of St. Gregory the Great: "My honour is the honour of the whole Church. My honour is the firm strength of my brethren. I am truly honoured when the honour due to each and all is not withheld."

Further, from this supreme power possessed by the Roman Pontiff of governing the universal Church, it follows that he has the right of free communication with the pastors of the whole Church, and with their flocks, that these may be taught and ruled by him in the way of salvation. Wherefore We con-

demn and reject the opinions of those who hold that the communication between this supreme head and the pastors and
their flocks can lawfully be impeded; or who make this communication subject to the will of the secular power, so as to
maintain that whatever is done by the Apostolic See, or by its
authority, for the government of the Church, cannot have force
or value unless it be confirmed by the assent of the secular
power.

And since by the divine right of apostolic primacy the Roman Pontiff is placed over the universal Church, We further
teach and declare that he is the supreme judge of the faithful,
and that in all causes, the decision of which belongs to the
Church, recourse may be had to his tribunal, and that none
may re-open the judgment of the Apostolic See, than whose
authority there is no greater, nor can any lawfully review its
judgment. Wherefore they err from the right course who assert
that it is lawful to appeal from the judgments of the Roman
Pontiffs to an ecumenical Council, as to an authority higher
than that of the Roman Pontiff.

If, then, any shall say that the Roman Pontiff has the office
merely of inspection or direction, and not full and supreme
power of jurisdiction over the universal Church, not only in
things which belong to faith and morals, but also in those
which relate to the discipline and government of the Church
spread throughout the world; or assert that he possesses merely
the principal part, and not the fullness of the supreme power;
or that this power which he enjoys is not ordinary and immediate, both over each and all the churches, and over each and
all the pastors of the faithful: let him be anathema.

CHAPTER IV

Concerning the Infallible Teaching
of the Roman Pontiff

Moreover, that the supreme power of teaching is also included in the apostolic primacy, which the Roman Pontiff, as
the successor of Peter, Prince of the Apostles, possesses over
the whole Church, this Holy See has always held, the perpetual practice of the Church confirms, and ecumenical Coun-

cils also have declared, especially those in which the East with the West met in the union of faith and charity. For the Fathers of the Fourth Council of Constantinople, following in the footsteps of their predecessors, gave forth this solemn profession: The first condition of salvation is to keep the rule of the true faith. And because the sentence of our Lord Jesus Christ cannot be passed by, who said: "Thou art Peter; and upon this rock I will build my Church," these things which have been said are approved by events, because in the Apostolic See the Catholic religion and her holy and well-known doctrine has always been kept undefiled. Desiring, therefore, not to be in the least degree separated from the faith and doctrine of that See, We hope that We may deserve to be in the one communion, which the Apostolic See preaches, in which is the entire and true solidity of the Christian religion. And, with the approval of the Second Council of Lyons, the Greeks professed that the holy Roman Church enjoys supreme and full primacy and pre-eminence over the whole Catholic Church, which it truly and humbly acknowledges in the person of blessed Peter, Prince or Head of the Apostles, whose successor the Roman Pontiff is; and as the Apostolic See is bound before all others to defend the truth of faith, so also, if any questions regarding faith shall arise, they must be defined by its judgment. Finally, the Council of Florence defined: That the Roman Pontiff is the true vicar of Christ, and the head of the whole Church, and the father and teacher of all Christians; and that to him in blessed Peter was delivered by our Lord Jesus Christ the full power of feeding, ruling, and governing the whole Church.

To satisfy this pastoral duty, our predecessors ever made unwearied efforts that the salutary doctrine of Christ might be propagated among all the nations of the earth, and with equal care watched that it might be preserved genuine and pure where it had been received. Therefore the Bishops of the whole world, now singly, now assembled in Synod, following the long-established custom of churches, and the form of the ancient rule, sent word to this Apostolic See of those dangers especially which sprang up in matters of faith, that there the losses of faith might be most effectually repaired where the faith cannot fail. And the Roman Pontiffs, according to the exigencies of times and circumstances, sometimes assembling ecumenical Councils, or asking for the mind of the Church scattered throughout the world, sometimes by particular Synods, sometimes using other helps which Divine Providence supplied, defined as to be held those things which with the help of God they had recognized as conformable with the sacred Scriptures and apostolic traditions. For the Holy Spirit was not promised to the successors of Peter, that by his revelation they might make known new doctrine; but that by his assistance they might inviolably keep and faithfully expound the revelation or deposit of faith delivered through the Apostles. And, indeed, all the venerable Fathers have embraced, and the holy orthodox doctors have venerated and followed, their apostolic doctrine; knowing most fully that this See of holy Peter remains ever free from all blemish of error according to the divine promise of the Lord our Saviour made to the Prince of his disciples: " I have prayed for thee that thy faith fail not, and when thou art converted, confirm thy brethren."

The gift, then, of truth and never-failing faith was conferred by heaven upon Peter and his successors in this chair, that they might perform their high office for the salvation of all; that the whole flock of Christ, kept away by them from the poisonous food of error, might be nourished with the pasture of heavenly doctrine; that the occasion of schism being removed, the whole Church might be kept one, and resting on its foundation, might stand firm against the gates of hell.

But since in this very age, in which the salutary efficacy of the apostolic office is most of all required, not a few are found who take away from its authority, We judge it altogether necessary solemnly to assert the prerogative which the only-begotten Son of God vouchsafed to join with the supreme pastoral office.

Therefore faithfully adhering to the tradition received from the beginning of the Christian faith, for the glory of God our Saviour, the exaltation of the Catholic religion, and the salvation of Christian people, the sacred Council approving, We teach and define that it is a dogma divinely revealed: that the

Roman Pontiff, when he speaks ex cathedra, that is, when in discharge of the office of pastor and doctor of all Christians, by virtue of his supreme apostolic authority, he defines a doctrine regarding faith or morals to be held by the universal Church, by the divine assistance promised to him in blessed Peter, is possessed of that infallibility with which the divine Redeemer willed that his Church should be endowed for defining doctrine regarding faith or morals; and that therefore such definitions of the Roman Pontiff are irreformable of themselves, and not from the consent of the Church.

But if any one — which may God avert — presume to contradict this our definition: let him be anathema.

Given at Rome in public Session solemnly held in the Vatican Basilica in the year of our Lord one thousand eight hundred and seventy, on the eighteenth day of July, in the twenty-fifth year of our Pontificate.

COMMENT AND EXPLICATION

Faith in Christ, the Church, and the Primacy

" Faith in the Church cannot stand pure and true without the support of faith in the primacy of the Bishop of Rome. The same moment when Peter, in the presence of all the Apostles and disciples, confessed his faith in Christ, Son of the Living God, the answer he received in reward for his faith and his confession was the word that built the Church, the only Church of Christ, on the rock of Peter (Matt. 16:18). Thus was sealed the connection between faith in Christ, the Church and the Primacy." Pius XI, *Mit brennender Sorge*, March 14, 1937.[5]

Power " to rule over the whole flock and each of its parts "

" The custom of consulting the Holy See, not only in doctrinal matters, but also in the affairs of government and discipline, has flourished from the earliest days of Christianity. . . . When asked for their decision, the Roman

Pontiffs did not answer as private theologians, but in virtue of their authority and conscious of the power which they received from Christ to rule over the whole flock and each of its parts. The same is deduced from the instances in which the Roman Pontiffs, unasked, settled disputes that had arisen or commanded that ' doubts ' be brought to them to be resolved.

" This union, therefore, and harmonious communication with the Holy See has arisen not from a kind of desire to centralize and unify everything, but by divine right and by reason of an essential element of the Constitution of the Church of Christ." Pius XII, *The Teaching Authority of the Church*, November 2, 1954.[6]

" The one true Church of Christ "

" The unity of Christians cannot be otherwise obtained than by securing the return of the separated to the one true Church of Christ from which they once unhappily withdrew, to the one true Church of Christ, standing forth before all and which by the will of its Founder will remain forever the same as when He Himself established it for the salvation of all mankind. The mystical Spouse of Christ has remained unspotted in the course of the centuries, nor can it ever be contaminated. . . . The mystical Body of Christ, this is to say, the Church, is, like the physical body, a unity. . . . Whoever, therefore, is not united with it is not a member of it nor does he communicate with its head, who is Christ." Pius XI, *Mortalium animos*, January 6, 1928.[7]

" The place of God Almighty "

" Since We hold upon this earth the place of God Almighty, who will have all men to be saved and to come to knowledge of the truth, and now that Our advanced age and the bitterness of anxious cares urge Us on towards the end common to every mortal, We feel drawn to follow the example of Our Redeemer and Master, Jesus Christ, who, when about to return to heaven, implored of God, his Father, . . . that his disciples and followers should be of one mind and of one heart." Leo XIII, *Praeclara gratulationis*, June 20, 1894.[8]

The duty of obedience

" In the one Church of Christ no one is found there and no one perseveres in it unless he recognizes and accepts obediently the supreme authority of St. Peter and his legitimate successors." Pius XI, *Mortalium animos*, January 6, 1928.[9]

" It is abhorent to the profession of a Christian for anyone to be unwilling to be subject and obedient to those who rule in the Church, and first of all to the bishops whom (without prejudice to the universal power of the Roman Pontiff) 'the Holy Ghost has placed to rule the Church of God which Christ has purchased by his blood.'"
Leo XIII, *Graves de communi*, January 18, 1901.[10]

Obedience due as to God himself

" Christians . . . receive their rule of faith from the Church, by whose authority and under whose guidance they are conscious that they have beyond question attained to truth. . . . Whatever things are manifestly revealed by God we must receive with similar and equal assent. To refuse to believe any one of them is equivalent to rejecting them all. . . . The supreme teacher in the Church is the Roman Pontiff. Union of minds, therefore, requires, together with a perfect accord in the one faith, complete submission and obedience to the Church and to the Roman Pontiff, as to God himself." Leo XIII, *Sapientiae christianae*, January 10, 1890.[11]

The distinguishing mark of Catholics

" This obedience should . . . be perfect, because it is enjoined by faith itself, and has this in common with faith, that it cannot be given in shreds; — nay, were it not absolute and perfect in every particular, it might wear the name of obedience, but its essence would disappear. Christian usage attaches such value to this perfection of obedience that it has been, and will ever be, accounted the distinguishing mark by which we are able to recognize Catholics." Leo XIII, *Sapientiae christianae*, January 10, 1890.[12]

" The multitude of the faithful . . . a docile flock "

" The Scripture teaches us, and the tradition of the Fathers confirms the teaching, that the Church is the mystical body of Christ, ruled by the *Pastors* and *Doctors* (Eph. 4:11 sqq.) — a society of men containing within its own fold chiefs who have full and perfect powers for ruling, teaching and judging. . . . It follows that the Church is essentially an unequal society, that is, a society comprising two categories of persons, the pastors and the flock, those who occupy a rank in the different degrees of the hierarchy and the multitude of the faithful. So distinct are these categories that with the pastoral body only rests the necessary right and authority for promoting the end of that society and directing all its members towards the end; the one duty of the multitude is to allow themselves to be led, and, like a docile flock, to follow the pastors." Pius X, *Vehementer Nos*, February 11, 1906.[13]

The teaching authority of the church

" God has given to his Church a living teaching authority to elucidate and explain what is contained in the deposit of faith only obscurely and implicitly. This deposit of faith our Divine Redeemer has given for authentic interpretation not to each of the faithful, not even to theologians, but only to the teaching authority of the Church." Pius XII, *Humani Generis,* August 12, 1950.[14]

" The office . . . of teaching lies by divine right in the province of the pastors, namely of the bishops whom *the Holy Ghost has placed to rule the Church of God.* It belongs above all to the Roman Pontiff, vicar of Jesus Christ, established as head of the universal Church, teacher of all that pertains to morals and faith." Leo XIII, *Sapientiae christianae,* January 10, 1890.[15]

Both what we are to believe and what we are to do
" The things contained in the divine oracles have reference to God in part, and in part to man, and to whatever is necessary for the attainment of eternal salvation. Now, both these, that is to say, what we are bound to believe and what we are obliged to do, are laid down . . . by the Church using her divine right, and in the Church by the Supreme Pontiff. Wherefore it belongs to the Pope to judge authoritatively what things the sacred oracles contain, as well as what doctrines are in harmony, and what in disagreement, with them; and also for the same reason, to show forth what things are to be accepted as right, and what to be rejected as worthless; what it is necessary to do and what to avoid doing, in order to attain eternal salvation." Leo XIII, *Sapientiae christianae,* January 10, 1890.[16]

Not only solemn judgments are to be obeyed
" Christ . . . has constituted the Church the guardian and the teacher of the whole of the truth concerning religion and moral conduct. To her, therefore, should the faithful show obedience and subject their minds and hearts so as to be kept unharmed and free from error and moral corruption; and so that they shall not deprive them-

selves of that assistance given by God with such liberal bounty, they ought to show this due obedience, not only when the Church defines something with solemn judgment, but also, in proper proportion, when, by the constitutions and decrees of the Holy See, opinions are proscribed and condemned as dangerous and distorted." Pius XI, *Casti connubi*, December 31, 1930.[17]

"It is quite foreign to everyone bearing the name of Christian to trust his own mental powers with such pride as to agree only with those things which he can examine from their inner nature, and to imagine that the Church, sent by God to teach and guide all nations, is not conversant with present affairs and circumstances, or even that they must obey only in those matters which she has decreed by means of solemn definition as though her other decisions might be presumed to be false. . . . Quite the contrary, a characteristic of all true followers of Christ, lettered or unlettered, is to suffer themselves to be guided and led in all things that touch upon faith and morals by the Holy Church of God, through its Supreme Pastor, the Roman Pontiff, who is himself guided by Jesus Christ Our Lord." Pius XI, *Casti connubi*, December 31, 1930.[18]

The binding authority of papal encyclicals
"What is expounded in the encyclical letters of the Roman Pontiffs concerning the nature and institution of the Church is deliberately and habitually neglected by some, with the idea of giving force to a certain vague notion which they profess to have been found in the ancient Fathers, especially the Greeks. The Popes, they assert, do not wish to pass judgment on what is a matter of dispute among theologians, so recourse must be had to the early sources, and the recent constitutions and decrees of the

teaching Church must be explained from the writings of the ancients.

"Although this seems well said, still it is not free from error. It is true that Popes generally leave theologians free in these matters which are disputed by reputable theologians; but history teaches that many matters that formerly were open to discussion no longer now admit of discussion.

"Nor must it be thought that what is expounded in encyclical letters does not itself demand consent, on the pretext that in writing such letters the Popes do not exercise the supreme power of their teaching authority. For these matters are taught with the ordinary teaching authority, of which it is true to say: 'He who heareth you, heareth me' (Luke 10:16); and generally what is expounded and inculcated in encyclical letters already for other reasons appertains to Catholic doctrine. But if the supreme Pontiffs in their official documents purposely pass judgment on a matter up to that time under dispute, it is obvious that the matter, according to the mind and will of the same Pontiffs, cannot be any longer considered a question open to discussion among theologians." Pius XII, *Humani Generis*, August 12, 1950.[19]

"In defining the limits of the obedience owed to the pastors of souls, but most of all to the authority of the Roman Pontiff, it must not be supposed that it is only to be yielded in relation to the dogmas of which the obstinate denial cannot be disjoined from the crime of heresy. Nay, further, it is not enough sincerely and firmly to assent to doctrines which, though not defined by any solemn pronouncement of the Church, are by her proposed to belief as divinely revealed in her common and universal teaching, and which the Vatican Council declared are to be be-

lieved *with Catholic and divine faith.* But this likewise
must be reckoned amongst the duties of Christians, that
they allow themselves to be ruled and directed by the
authority and leadership of bishops, and above all of the
Apostolic See." Leo XIII, *Sapientiae christianae,* January
10, 1890.[20]

The authority of the church is not limited to "matters strictly religious"

"There are some noticeable attitudes and tendencies
of mind which presume to check and set limits to the
power of Bishops (the Roman Pontiff not excepted). . . .
They fix their authority, office and watchfulness within
certain bounds, which concern strictly religious matters,
the statement of the truths of the faith, the regulation of
devotional practices, administration of the Sacraments of
the Church, and the carrying out of liturgical ceremonies.
They wish to restrain the Church from all undertakings
and business which concern life as it is really conducted —
' the realities of life,' as they say. In short, this way of thinking in the official statements of some lay Catholics, even
those in high positions, is sometimes shown when they say:
' We are perfectly willing to see, to listen to and to approach Bishops and priests in their churches, and regarding matters within their authority; but in places of official
and public business, where matters of this life are dealt
with and decided, we have no wish to see them or to listen
to what they say. For there, it is we laymen, and not the
clergy — no matter of what rank or qualification — who
are the legitimate judges.'

"We must take an open and firm stand against errors
of this kind. The power of the Church is not bound by the
limits of 'matters strictly religious,' as they say, but the

whole matter of the natural law, its foundation, its interpretation, its application, so far as their moral aspects extend, are within the Church's power. For the keeping of the natural law, by God's appointment, has reference to the road by which man has to approach his supernatural end. But, on this road, the Church is man's guide and guardian in what concerns his supreme end. . . . Therefore, when it is a question of instructions and propositions which the properly constituted shepherds (i.e., the Roman Pontiff for the whole Church and the Bishops for the faithful entrusted to them) publish on matters within the natural law, the faithful must not invoke that saying (which is wont to be employed with respect to opinions of individuals): 'the strength of the authority is no more than the strength of the arguments.'

" Hence, even though to someone certain declarations of the Church may not seem proved by the arguments put forward, his obligation to obey still remains. . . .

" Many and serious are the problems in the social field. Whether they be merely social or socio-political, they pertain to the moral order, are of concern to conscience and the salvation of men; thus they cannot be declared outside the authority and care of the Church. Indeed, there are problems outside the social field, not strictly 'religious,' political problems, of concern either to individual nations, or to all nations, which belong to the moral order, weigh on the conscience and can, and very often do, hinder the attainment of man's last end. Such are the purpose and limits of temporal authority; the relations between the individuals and society; the so-called 'totalitarian state,' whatever be the principle it is based on; the 'complete laicization of the state' and of public life; the complete laicization of the schools; war, its morality, liceity or nonliceity when waged as it is today, and whether a conscientious person may give or withhold his co-operation in it; the moral relationships which bind and rule the various nations.

" Common sense, and truth as well, are contradicted by whoever asserts that these and like problems are outside the field of morals, and hence . . . beyond the influence of that authority established by God. . . .

" Clergy and the laity must realize that the Church is fitted and authorized . . . to promote ecclesiastical discipline and see to its observance, i.e., to establish an external norm of action and conduct for matters which concern public order and which do not have their immediate origin in natural or divine law. Clerics and the laity may not exempt themselves from this discipline. . . .

" Not a few moderns, men and women, think that the leadership and vigilance of the Church is not to be suffered by one who is grown up; they not only say it, but they hold it as a firm conviction. . . . They wish to be treated as adults who are in full possession of their rights, and can decide for themselves what they must, or must not, do in any given situation.

" Let the Church — they do not hesitate to say — propose her doctrine, pass her laws as norms of our actions. Still, when there is question of practical application to each individual's life, the Church must not interfere; she should let each one of the faithful follow his own conscience and judgment. . . .

" Two years ago . . . , We spoke about these reprehensible theories. . . . Concerning the importance given to the attainment of a person's majority, this assertion is correct; it is just and right that adults should not be ruled as children. . . . But to be an adult and to have put off the things of childhood is one thing, and quite another to be an adult and not to be subject to the guidance and government of legitimate authority." Pius XII, *The Teaching Authority of the Church*, November 2, 1954.[21]

The right and duty to deal authoritatively with social and economic questions

" Before proceeding to discuss these problems We lay down the principle long since clearly established by Leo XIII that it is Our right and Our duty to deal authoritatively with social and economic problems. It is not, of course, the office of the Church to lead men to transient and perishable happiness only, but to that which is eternal. . . . But she never can relinquish her God-given task of interpreting her authority, not, indeed, in technical matters, of which she has neither the equipment nor the mission, but in all those that have a bearing on moral conduct. For the deposit of truth entrusted to Us by God, and Our weighty office of propagating, interpreting and urging in season and out of season the entire moral law, demand that both social and economic questions be brought within Our supreme jurisdiction, in so far as they refer to moral issues." Pius XI, *Quadragesimo anno*, May 15, 1931.[22]

The teachings of Leo XIII and his successors remain in full force

" Many believe in or claim that they believe in and hold fast to Catholic doctrine on such questions as social authority, the right of owning private property, on the relations between capital and labor, on the rights of the laboring man, on the relations between Church and State, religion and country, on the relations between the different social classes, on international relations, on the rights of the Holy See and the prerogatives of the Roman Pontiff and the Episcopate, on the social rights of Jesus Christ, who is the Creator, Redeemer, and Lord not only of individuals but of nations. In spite of these protestations, they speak, write, and, what is more, act, as if it were not necessary any longer to follow, or that they did not remain still in full force, the teachings and solemn pronouncements which may be found in so many documents of the Holy See, and particularly in those written by Leo XIII, Pius X, and Benedict XV." Pius XI, *Ubi arcano,* December 23, 1922.[23]

A caution to be observed

" If the Church does exercise this function of teaching, as she often has through the centuries, either in the ordinary or extraordinary way, it is clear how false is a procedure which would attempt to explain what is clear by means of what is obscure. Indeed the very opposite procedure must be used. Hence our predecessor of immortal memory, Pius IX, teaching that the most noble office of theology is to show how a doctrine defined by the Church is contained in the sources of revelation, added these words, and with very good reason: ' In that sense in which it has been defined by the Church.' . . . For some go so far as to . . . judge the doctrine of the Fathers and of the teaching Church by the norm of holy Scripture, interpreted by the purely human reason or exegesis, instead of explaining holy Scripture according to the mind of the Church which Christ our Lord has appointed guardian and interpreter of the whole deposit of divinely revealed truth. . . .

" It is not surprising that novelties of this kind have already borne their deadly fruit in almost all branches of theology. It is now doubted that human reason, without divine revelation and the help of divine grace, can, by arguments drawn from the created universe, prove the existence of a personal God. . . . Some also question whether angels are personal beings. . . . Nor is this all. . . . Some say they are not bound by the doctrine, explained in our encyclical letter of a few years ago and based on the sources of revelation, which teaches that the mystical body of Christ and the Roman Catholic Church are one and the same thing. Some reduce to a meaningless formula the necessity of belonging to the true Church in order to gain salvation. . . .

" These and like errors, it is clear, have crept in among certain of our sons who are deceived by imprudent zeal for souls or by false science. . . . For this reason, after mature reflection and consideration before God, that We may not be wanting in our sacred duty, We charge Bishops and superiors general of religious orders, binding them most seriously in conscience, to take the most diligent care that such opinions be not advanced in schools, in conferences, or in writings of any kind, and that they be not taught in any manner whatsoever to the clergy or the faithful.

" Let teachers in ecclesiastical institutions be aware that they cannot with tranquil conscience exercise the office of teaching entrusted to them unless in the instruction of their students they religiously accept and exactly observe the norms which we have ordained. That due reverence and submission which in their unceasing labor they must profess toward the teaching authority of the Church, let them instill also into the minds and hearts of their students." Pius XII, *Humani Generis,* August 12, 1950.[24]

Security measures to be adopted

" Care of all the Church, and the daily vigilance which Our supreme office demands of Us, compel Us to consider and weigh certain ideas, sentiments, and ways of acting. We draw your attention to them, and ask you to unite your vigilant care with Ours, in order thus to provide more quickly and effectively for the needs of Christ's flock. There are evident the symptoms and effects of a certain spiritual contagion, which require your pastoral care, in order that they may not spread, but may be remedied in time and extirpated. . . .

" Bishops . . . retain the very grave obligation of supervising the doctrine, which others propose, in order to help them, and of seeing to its integrity and security. Therefore the legitimate Teaching Authority of the Church is guilty of no injury or no offense to any of those to whom it has given a canonical mission [to teach], if it desires to ascertain what they, to whom it has entrusted the mission of teaching, are proposing and defending in their lectures, in books, notes and reviews intended for the use of their students, as well as in books and other publications intended for the general public. In order to accomplish this, We do not contemplate extending the prescriptions of canon law on previous censorship of books to include all these kinds of teaching; for there are many ways and means at hand for investigating and acquiring accurate information on what professors are teaching.[25] And this care and prudence of the legitimate Teaching Authority does not at all imply distrust or suspicion — (nor does the profession of faith which the Church requires of professors and many others; cf. *Canon 1406*, nn. 7 f.) — on the contrary, the fact that the office of teacher has been bestowed implies confidence, high regard, and honor shown the per-

son to whom the office has been entrusted. Indeed the
Holy See, whenever it inquires and wishes to be informed
about what is being taught in various seminaries, colleges,
universities, and institutions of higher learning, in those
fields which pertain to its jurisdiction, is led by no other
motive than the consciousness of Christ's mandate and the
obligation by which She is bound before God to safeguard
and preserve without corruption or adulteration sound
doctrine." Pius XII, *Si diligis*, address to the Cardinals,
Archbishops, and Bishops assembled for the canonization
of Piux X, May 31, 1954.[26]

The role of the Apostolic Delegate in the United States
"When the Council of Baltimore had concluded its
labors, the duty still remained of putting, so to speak, a
proper and becoming crown upon the work. This, We perceived, could scarcely be done in a more fitting manner
than through the due establishment by the Apostolic See
of an American Legation. Accordingly, as you are well
aware, We have done this. By this action, . . . We had
in mind to draw more closely the bonds of duty and friend-
ship which connect you and so many thousands of Catholics with the Apostolic See. . . . It has been, from earliest
antiquity, the custom of the Roman Pontiffs in the exercise of the divinely bestowed gift of the primacy in the
administration of the Church of Christ to send forth legates
to Christian nations and peoples. And they did this, not by
an adventitious but an inherent right. For 'the Roman
Pontiff, upon whom Christ has conferred ordinary and immediate jurisdiction, as well over all and singular churches,
as over all and singular pastors and faithful (Dogmatic
Constitution of the Church, Chapter III), since he cannot
personally visit the different regions and thus exercise the

pastoral office over the flock entrusted to him, finds it
necessary, from time to time, in the discharge of the ministry imposed on him, to dispatch legates into different
parts of the world, according as the need arises; who,
supplying his place, may correct errors, make the rough
ways plain, and administer to the people confided to their
care increased means of salvation.'

" But how unjust and baseless would be the suspicion
should it anywhere exist, that the powers conferred on the
legate are an obstacle to the authority of the bishops!
Sacred to Us (more than to any other) are the rights of
those ' *whom the Holy Ghost has placed as bishops to rule
the Church of God.*' That these rights should remain intact
in every nation and in every part of the globe, We both
desire and ought to desire, the more so since the dignity
of the individual bishop is by nature so interwoven with
the dignity of the Roman Pontiff that any measure which
benefits the one necessarily protects the other. . . .
Therefore, since it is the office and function of an apostolic
legate, with whatsoever powers he may be vested, to exe-
cute the mandates and interpret the will of the Pontiff
who sends him, thus, so far from his being of any detriment to the ordinary power of bishops, he will rather
bring an accession of stability and strength. His authority
will possess no slight weight for preserving in the multitude a submissive spirit; in the clergy discipline and due
reverence for the bishops and in the bishops mutual
charity and an intimate union of souls. And since this
union, so salutary and desirable, consists mainly in harmony of thought and action, he will, no doubt, bring it
to pass that each one of you shall persevere in the diligent
administration of his diocesan affairs; that one shall not
impede another in matters of government; that one shall

not pry into the counsels and conduct of another; finally, that with disagreements eradicated and mutual esteem maintained, you may all work together with combined energies to promote the glory of the American Church and the general welfare. . . . What is the meaning of the legation of which We are speaking, or what is its ultimate aim except to bring it about that the constitution of the Church shall be strengthened, her discipline better fortified? Wherefore, We ardently desire that this truth should sink day by day more deeply into the minds of Catholics — namely, that they can in no better way safeguard their own individual interests and the common good than by yielding a hearty submission and obedience to the Church." Leo XIII, *Longinqua oceani,* January 6, 1895.[27]

III

THE CHRISTIAN CONSTITUTION
OF STATES

THE basic structure of Roman Catholic political theory
is authoritatively set forth in the encyclical letters of
Leo XIII (1878–1903), most notably and comprehensively
in "The Christian Constitution of States" (*Immortale
Dei*), which he issued for the instruction of the faithful on
November 1, 1885.[1] Leo's predecessor, Pius IX (1846–
1878), had set the Roman Church firmly and unyieldingly
against the tide of democratic sentiment that had been
sweeping across Europe and transforming the old regimes
into limited constitutional monarchies. The unification of
Italy under Cavour's slogan of "A free church in a free
state" was a particularly bitter blow, and Pius IX — in a
gesture of protest — withdrew into a voluntary "imprison-
ment" within the Vatican. The policies of Pius IX quite
obviously were a failure, succeeding only in rendering the
Roman Church increasingly isolated and ineffective in
political affairs.

As a "liberal" Pope, Leo XIII saw it as his great task
to reverse the trend toward isolation from the centers of
political power. To do this, he had to do two things. The
first was to redefine the political theory of Roman Catholicism, which had been almost completely oriented to

princely and authoritarian rule. Leo had to find some way, within the basic dogmatic structure of the church, by which Roman Catholic political theory could at least partially adjust itself to the new conditions in which the church was forced to operate. He also recognized that it was necessary to replace the instructions that prohibited the faithful from participating in the political life of certain regimes with more positive counsel. With this in mind, he stressed the importance of politics and pointed out to the faithful how and to what extent they could both faithfully and effectively engage in political activities within democratic states; and in doing so he sketched the chief features of what was to become known as Catholic Action.

"It is not difficult," he said, "to determine what would be the form and character of the State were it governed according to the principles of Christian philosophy." While "the right to rule" is not tied to "any special mode of government," yet the government must be of such a nature as to recognize God as the source of its authority and to "insure the general welfare." This means that a properly constituted state must make a "public profession" of "the religion which God enjoins," and must foster, promote, and protect it. It also means a firm rejection of any notion of popular sovereignty, of government by the consent of the governed, and of the prince as a delegate of the people; for the powers of the ruling authority are from God and not from the people. Above all, the properly constituted state must safeguard the "true liberty" of its people by firmly rejecting the pernicious notions of freedom of religion, freedom of speech, freedom of assembly, and freedom of the press.

Side by side with the state is the church. While the state

is designed to serve the temporal needs of men, the church is a society chartered by divine right to bring men safely to their ultimate end. God has willed that both state and church should be free to exercise their authority within the respective spheres of their own competence; and he has also willed that they should exist and function in perfect harmony. But " inasmuch as each of these two powers has authority over the same subjects," it not infrequently occurs that the same matter may belong to " the jurisdiction and determination of both." Under such circumstances, in order that there may be no conflict, God has willed that the church, since it serves the noblest of ends and possesses the most exalted of all authority, shall take precedence. Furthermore, since the church must be " unhampered," " unfettered," and " unimpeded " in the exercise of its powers, it is for the church to determine, " in accordance with her own judgment, all matters that fall within her competence."

This is the statement of the theory, of the norm, of the goal to be sought; but Leo acknowledged that, due to particular circumstances in any given nation, a full Christian organization of society may not always be either possible or practical. Under certain conditions, the church will not judge it " blameworthy " for " the people to have a share, greater or less, in the government." Indeed, at certain times and under certain conditions, " such participation may not only be of benefit to the citizens, but may even be of obligation." Furthermore, while the church " deems it unlawful to place the various forms of Divine Worship on the same footing as the true religion," it does not, " on that account, condemn those rulers who, for the sake of securing some great good or of hindering some great evil, tolerate in practice that these various forms of religion have a place in the State." Thus, when circumstances make such concessions necessary, "the Church gives signal proof of her motherly love by showing the greatest possible kindliness and indulgence."

The duties of Roman Catholics " in these difficult times in which our lot is cast " are as follows: First, to hold with " a firm grasp of mind " all that " the Roman Pontiffs have hitherto taught, or shall hereafter teach." It is especially necessary that, " with reference to the so-called ' Liberties ' which are so greatly coveted in these days, all must stand by the judgment of the Apostolic See, and have the same mind." Secondly, in private and domestic affairs, it is incumbent upon them " to conform life and conduct to the gospel precepts, and to refuse to shrink from this duty when Christian virtue demands some sacrifice difficult to make." They are " to love the Church as their common mother, to obey her laws, promote her honor, defend her rights, and to endeavor to make her respected and loved by those over whom they have authority." Thirdly, except under the exceptional conditions which prevailed in Italy, " it is the duty of all Catholics worthy of the name " to take an active part in politics, making " use of popular institutions " in an endeavor " to bring back all civil society to the pattern and form of Christianity which We have described." While different methods to achieve this goal must be adopted in different situations, they must be pursued under " the guidance of the Apostolic See " and in obedience to " the bishops whom the Holy Ghost has placed ' to rule the Church of God.' "

With this brief summary by way of introduction, we turn to the document itself, which was addressed to the Patriarchs, Primates, Archbishops, and Bishops in communion with the Apostolic See.

Encyclical Letter of Leo XIII, November 1, 1885
on

THE CHRISTIAN CONSTITUTION OF STATES [2]

The Catholic Church, that imperishable handiwork of our all-merciful God, has for her immediate and natural purpose the saving of souls and securing our happiness in heaven. Yet in regard to things temporal she is the source of benefits as manifold and great as if the chief end of her existence were to ensure the prospering of our earthly life. And in truth, wherever the Church has set her foot, she has straightway changed the face of things, and has attempered the moral tone of the people with a new civilization, and with virtues before unknown. All nations which have yielded to her sway have become eminent for the culture, their sense of justice, and the glory of their high deeds.

And yet a hackneyed reproach of old date is leveled against her, that the Church is opposed to the rightful aims of the civil government, and is wholly unable to afford help in spreading that welfare and progress which justly and naturally are sought after by every well-regulated State. From the very beginning Christians were harassed by slanderous accusations of this nature, and on that account were held up to hatred and execration, for being (so they were called) enemies of the empire. The Christian religion was moreover commonly charged with being the cause of the calamities that so frequently befell the State, whereas, in very truth, just punishment was being awarded to guilty nations by an avenging God. This odious calumny, with most valid reason, nerved the genius and sharpened the pen of St. Augustine, who, notably in his treatise *On the City of God,* set forth in so bright a light the worth of Christian wisdom in its relation to the public weal, that he seems not merely to have pleaded the cause of the Christians of his day, but to have refuted for all future times impeachments so grossly contrary to truth. The wicked proneness, however, to levy the like charges and accusations has not been lulled to rest.

Many, indeed, are they who have tried to work out a plan

of civil society based on doctrines other than those approved by the Catholic Church. Nay, in these latter days a novel scheme of law has begun in many places to be held and to have influence, the outcome, as it is maintained of an age arrived at full stature, and the result of progressive liberty. But though endeavors of various kinds have been ventured on, it is clear that no better mode has been devised for the building up and ruling the State than that which is the necessary growth of the teachings of the Gospel. We deem it, therefore, of the highest moment, and a strict duty of Our Apostolic office, to contrast with the lessons taught by Christ the novel theories now advanced touching the State. By this means We cherish hope that the bright shining of the truth may scatter the mists of error and doubt, so that one and all may see clearly the imperious law of life which they are bound to follow and obey.

The true Christian organization of civil society

It is not difficult to determine what would be the form and character of the State were it governed according to the principles of Christian philosophy. Man's natural instinct moves him to live in civil society, for he cannot, if dwelling apart, provide himself with the necessary requirements of life, nor procure the means of developing his mental and moral faculties. Hence it is divinely ordained that he should lead his life — be it family, social, or civil — with his fellow men, amongst whom alone his several wants can be adequately supplied. But as no society can hold together unless some one be over all, directing all to strive earnestly for the common good; every civilized community must have a ruling authority, and this authority, no less than society itself, has its source in nature, and has, consequently, God for its author. Hence it follows that all public power must proceed from God: for God alone is the true and supreme Lord of the world. Everything, without exception, must be subject to Him, and must serve Him, so that whosoever holds the right to govern, holds it from the one sole and single source, namely, God, the Sovereign Ruler of all. "There is no power but from God." (Rom. 13:1.)

The right to rule is not necessarily, however, bound up with any special mode of government. It may take this or that form, provided only that it be of a nature to insure the general welfare. But whatever be the nature of the government, rulers must ever bear in mind that God is the paramount Ruler of the world, and must set Him before themselves as their exemplar and law in the administration of the State. For, in things visible, God has fashioned secondary causes, in which His divine action can in some wise be discerned, leading up to the end to which the course of the world is ever tending. In like manner in civil society, God has always willed that there should be a ruling authority, and that they who are invested with it should reflect the divine power and providence in some measure over the human race.

They, therefore, who rule should rule with evenhanded justice, not as masters, but rather as fathers, for the rule of God over man is most just, and is tempered always with a father's kindness. Government should, moreover, be administered for the well-being of the citizens because they who govern others possess authority solely for the welfare of the State. Furthermore, the civil power must not be subservient to the advantage of any one individual or of some few persons, inasmuch as it was established for the common good of all. But if those who are in authority rule unjustly, if they govern overbearingly or arrogantly, and if their measures prove hurtful to the people, they must remember that the Almighty will one day bring them to account, the more strictly in proportion to the sacredness of their office and pre-eminence of their dignity. "The mighty shall be mightily tormented." (Wisd. of Sol. 6:7.) Then truly will the majesty of the law meet with the dutiful and willing homage of the people, when they are convinced that their rulers hold authority from God, and feel that it is a matter of justice and duty to obey them, and to show them reverence and fealty, united to a love not unlike that which children show their parents. "Let every soul be subject to higher powers." (Rom. 13:1.) To despise legitimate authority, in whomsoever vested, is unlawful, as a rebellion against the Divine Will, and whoever resists that, rushes willfully to destruction. "He that resisteth the power, resisteth the ordinance of God, and they that resist, purchase to themselves damnation." (Rom. 13:2.) To cast aside obedience, and by popular violence to incite to revolt, is therefore treason, not against man only, but against God.

As a consequence, the State, constituted as it is, is clearly bound to act up to the manifold and weighty duties linking it to God by the public profession of religion. Nature and reason, which command every individual devoutly to worship God in holiness, because we belong to Him and must return to Him since from Him we came, bind also the civil community by a like law. For men living together in society are under the power of God no less than individuals are, and society, not less than individuals, owes gratitude to God, who gave it being and maintains it, and whose ever-bounteous goodness enriches it with countless blessings. Since, then, no one is allowed to be remiss in the service due to God, and since the chief duty of all men is to cling to religion in both its teaching and practice — not such religion as they may have a preference for, but the religion which God enjoins, and which certain and most clear marks show to be the only one true religion — it is a public crime to act as though there were no God. So, too, is it a sin in the State not to have care for religion, as a something beyond its scope, or as of no practical benefit; or out of many forms of religion to adopt that one which chimes in with the fancy; for we are bound absolutely to worship God in that way which He has shown to be His will. All who rule, therefore, should hold in honor the holy Name of God, and one of their chief duties must be to favor religion, to protect it, to shield it under the credit and sanction of the laws, and neither to organize nor enact any measures that may compromise its safety. This is the bounden duty of rulers to the people over whom they rule: for one and all we are destined, by our birth and adoption, to enjoy, when this frail and fleeting life is ended, a supreme and final good in heaven, and to the attainment of this every endeavor should be directed. Since, then, upon this depends the full and perfect happiness of mankind, the securing of this end should be of all imaginable interests the most urgent. Hence civil society, established for the common welfare, should not only safeguard the well-being of the community, but have also at heart the interests of its individual members, in such mode as not in any way to hinder, but in every manner to render as easy as may be, the possession of that highest and unchangeable good for which all should seek. Wherefore, for this purpose, care must especially be taken to preserve unharmed and unimpeded the religion whereof the practice is the link connecting man with God.

Now, it cannot be difficult to find out which is the true religion, if only it be sought with an earnest and unbiased mind; for proofs are abundant and striking. We have, for example, the fulfillment of prophecies; miracles in great number; the rapid spread of the faith in the midst of enemies and in face of overwhelming obstacles; the witness of the martyrs, and the like. From all these it is evident that the only true religion is the one established by Jesus Christ Himself, and which He committed to His Church to protect and to propagate.

For the only-begotten Son of God established on earth a society which is called the Church, and to it He handed over the exalted and divine office which He had received from His Father, to be continued through the ages to come. "As the Father hath sent Me, I also send you." (John 20:21.) "Behold I am with you, all days, even to the consummation of the world." (Matt. 28:20.) Consequently, as Jesus Christ came into the world that men "might have life and have it more abundantly" (John 10:10), so also has the Church for its aim and end the eternal salvation of souls, and hence it is so constituted as to open wide its arms to all mankind, unhampered by any limit of either time or place. "Preach ye the Gospel to every creature." (Mark 16:15.)

Over this mighty multitude God has Himself set rulers with power to govern; and He has willed that one should be the head of all, and the chief and unerring teacher of truth, to whom He has given "the keys of the kingdom of heaven" (Matt. 16:19). "Feed My lambs, feed My sheep." (John 21:16-17.) "I have prayed for thee that thy faith fail not." (Luke 22:32.)

This society is made up of men, just as civil society is, and yet is supernatural and spiritual, on account of the end for which it was founded, and of the means by which it aims at attaining that end. Hence it is distinguished and differs from civil society; and what is of highest moment, it is a society chartered as of right divine, perfect in its nature and in its title, to possess in itself and by itself, through the will and loving-kindness of its Founder, all needful provision for its maintenance and action. And just as the end at which the Church aims is by far the noblest of ends, so is its authority the most exalted of all authority, nor can it be looked upon as inferior to the civil power, or in any manner dependent upon it.

In very truth Jesus Christ gave to His apostles unrestrained authority in regard to things sacred, together with the genuine and most true power of making laws, as also with the twofold right of judging and of punishing, which flow from that power. "All power is given to Me in heaven and in earth: going therefore, teach ye all nations . . . teaching them to observe all things whatsoever I have commanded you." (Matt. 28:18-20.) And in another place, "If he will not hear them, tell the Church" (Matt. 18:17). And again, "In readiness to revenge all disobedience" (II Cor. 10:6). And once more, "That . . . I may not deal more severely according to the power which the Lord hath given me, unto edification and not unto destruction" (II Cor. 13:10). Hence it is the Church, and not the State, that is to be man's guide to heaven. It is to the Church that God had assigned the charge of seeing to, and legislating for, all that concerns religion; of teaching all nations; of spreading the Christian faith as widely as possible; in short, of administering freely and without hindrance, in accordance with her own judgment, all matters that fall within her competence.

Now this authority, perfect in itself, and plainly meant to be unfettered, so long assailed by a philosophy that truckles to the State, the Church has never ceased to claim for herself and openly to exercise. The Apostles themselves were the first to uphold it, when, being forbidden by the rulers of the Synagogue to preach the Gospel, they courageously answered, "We ought to obey God rather than men" (Acts 5:29). This same authority the holy Fathers of the Church were always careful to maintain by weighty arguments, according as occasion arose, and the Roman Pontiffs have never shrunk from

defending it with unbending constancy. Nay more, princes and
all invested with power to rule have themselves approved it,
in theory alike and in practice. It cannot be called in question
that in the making of treaties, in the transaction of business
matters, in the sending and receiving ambassadors, and in the
interchange of other kinds of official dealings, they have been
wont to treat with the Church as with a supreme and legitimate power. And assuredly all ought to hold that it was not
without a singular disposition of God's providence, that this
power of the Church was provided with a civil sovereignty as
the surest safeguard of her independence.

The Almighty, therefore, has appointed the charge of the
human race between two powers, the ecclesiastical and the
civil, the one being set over divine, and the other over human,
things. Each in its kind is supreme, each has fixed limits within
which it is contained, limits which are defined by the nature
and special object of the province of each, so that there is, we
may say, an orbit traced out within which the action of each is
brought into play by its own native right. But inasmuch as
each of these two powers has authority over the same subjects, and as it might come to pass that one and the same thing
— related differently, but still remaining one and the same
thing — might belong to the jurisdiction and determination of
both, therefore God, who foresees all things, and who is the
Author of these two powers, has marked out the course of
each in right correlation to the other. "For the powers that
are, are ordained of God." (Rom. 13:1.) Were this not so, deplorable contentions and conflicts would often arise, and not
infrequently men, like travelers at the meeting of two roads,
would hesitate in anxiety and doubt, not knowing what course
to follow. Two powers would be commanding contrary things,
and it would be a dereliction of duty to disobey either of the
two.

But it would be most repugnant to deem thus of the wisdom
and goodness of God. Even in physical things, albeit of a
lower order, the Almighty has so combined the forces and
springs of Nature with tempered action and wondrous harmony, that no one of them clashes with any other, and all of
them most fitly and aptly work together for the great pur-

pose of the universe. There must, accordingly, exist, between these two powers, a certain orderly connection, which may be compared to the union of the soul and body in man. The nature and scope of that connection can be determined only, as We have laid down, by having regard to the nature of each power, and by taking account of the relative excellence and nobleness of their purpose. One of the two has for its proximate and chief object the well-being of this mortal life; the other the everlasting joys of heaven. Whatever, therefore, in things human is of a sacred character, whatever belongs either of its own nature or by reason of the end to which it is referred, to the salvation of souls, or to the worship of God, is subject to the power and judgment of the Church. Whatever is to be ranged under the civil and political order is rightly subject to the civil authority. Jesus Christ has Himself given command that what is Caesar's is to be rendered to Caesar, and that what belongs to God is to be rendered to God.

There are, nevertheless, occasions when another method of concord is available for the sake of peace and liberty: We mean when rulers of the State and the Roman Pontiff come to an understanding touching some special matter. At such times the Church gives signal proof of her motherly love by showing the greatest possible kindliness and indulgence.

Such then, as We have briefly pointed out, is the Christian organization of civil society; not rashly or fancifully shaped out, but educed from the highest and truest principles, confirmed by natural reason itself.

The abundant benefits to civil society

In such an organization of the State, there is nothing that can be thought to infringe upon the dignity of rulers, and nothing unbecoming them; nay, so far from degrading the sovereign power in its due rights, it adds to its permanence and luster. Indeed, when more fully pondered, this mutual co-ordination has a perfection in which all other forms of government are lacking, and from which excellent results would flow, were the several component parts to keep their place, and duly discharge the office and work appointed respectively for each. And, without a doubt, in the constitution of the State such as we have described, divine and human things are equitably shared; the rights of citizens assured to them, and fenced round by divine, by natural, and by human law; the duties incumbent on each one being wisely marked out, and their fulfillment fittingly ensured. In their uncertain and toilsome journey toward "the city made without hands," all see that they have safe guides and helpers on their way, and are conscious that others have charge to protect their persons alike and their possessions, and to obtain or preserve for them everything essential for their present life. Furthermore, domestic society acquires that firmness and solidity so needful to it, from the holiness of marriage, one and indissoluble, wherein the rights and duties of husband and wife are controlled with wise justice and equity; due honor is assured to the woman; the authority of the husband is conformed to the pattern afforded by the authority of God; the power of the father is tempered by a due regard for the dignity of the mother and her offspring; and the best possible provision is made for the guardianship, welfare, and education of the children.

In political affairs, and all matters civil, the laws aim at securing the common good, and are not framed according to the delusive caprices and opinions of the mass of the people, but by truth and by justice; the ruling powers are invested with a sacredness more than human, and are withheld from deviating from the path of duty, and from overstepping the bounds of rightful authority; and the obedience of citizens is rendered with a feeling of honor and dignity, since obedience is not the servitude of man to man, but submission to the will of God, exercising His sovereignty through the medium of men. Now, this being recognized as undeniable, it is felt that the high office of rulers should be held in respect; that public authority should be constantly and faithfully obeyed; that no act of sedition should be committed; and that the civic order of the commonwealth should be maintained as sacred.

So, also, as to the duties of each one toward his fellow men, mutual forbearance, kindliness, generosity, are placed in the ascendant; the man who is at once a citizen and a Christian is not drawn aside by conflicting obligations; and, lastly, the abundant benefits with which the Christian religion, of its very nature, endows even the mortal life of man, are acquired for the community and civil society. And this to such an extent that it may be said in sober truth: " The condition of the commonwealth depends on the religion with which God is worshiped: and between one and the other there exists an intimate and abiding connection" (*Sacr. Im. ad Cyrillum Alexand. et Episcopos Metrop.* Cfr. Labbe, *Collect. Conc.*, T. iii).

Admirably, according to his wont, does St. Augustine, in many passages, enlarge upon the potency of these advantages; but nowhere more markedly and to the point than when he addresses the Catholic Church in the following words: " Thou dost teach and train children with much tenderness, young men with much vigor, old men with much gentleness; as the age not of the body alone, but of the mind of each requires. Women thou dost subject to their husbands in chaste and faithful obedience, not for the gratifying of their lust, but for bringing forth children, and having a share in the family concerns. Thou dost set husbands over their wives, not that they may plan false to the weaker sex, but according to the requirements of sincere affection. Thou dost subject children to their parents in a kind of free service, and dost establish parents over their children with a benign rule. . . . Thou joinest together, not in society only, but in a sort of brotherhood, citizen with citizen, nation with nation, and the whole race of men, by reminding them of their common parentage. Thou teachest kings to look to the interests of their people, and dost admonish the people to be submissive to their kings. With all care dost thou teach all to whom honor is due, and affection, and reverence, and fear, consolation, and admonition and exhortation, and discipline, and reproach, and punishment. Thou showest that all these are not equally incumbent on all, but that charity is owing to all, and wrongdoing to none" (*De moribus Eccl. Cathol.*, xxx. 63). And in another place, blaming the false wisdom of certain timesaving philosophers, he observes: " Let those who say that the teaching of Christ is hurtful to the State, produce such armies as the maxims of Jesus have enjoined soldiers to bring into being;

such governors of provinces; such husbands and wives; such parents and children; such masters and servants; such kings; such judges, and such payers and collectors of tribute, as the Christian teaching instructs them to become, and then let them dare to say that such teaching is hurtful to the State. Nay, rather will they hesitate to own that this discipline, if duly acted up to, is the very mainstay of the commonwealth? " (*Epist. 138*, al. 5, *ad Marcellinum*, ii, 15).

There was once a time when States were governed by the principles of Gospel teaching. Then it was that the power and divine virtue of Christian wisdom had diffused itself throughout the laws, institutions, and morals of the people; permeating all ranks and relations of civil society. Then, too, the religion instituted by Jesus Christ, established firmly in befitting dignity, flourished everywhere, by the favor of princes and the legitimate protection of magistrates; and Church and State were happily united in concord and friendly interchange of good offices.

The State, constituted in this wise, bore fruits important beyond all expectation, whose remembrance is still, and always will be, in renown, witnessed to as they are by countless proofs which can never be blotted out or even obscured by any craft of any enemies. Christian Europe has subdued barbarous nations, and changed them from a savage to a civilized condition, from superstition to true worship. It victoriously rolled back the tide of Mohammedan conquest; retained the headship of civilization; stood forth in the front rank as the leader and teacher of all, in every branch of national culture; bestowed on the world the gift of true and many-sided liberty; and most wisely founded very numerous institutions for the solace of human suffering. And if we inquire how it was able to bring about so altered a condition of things, the answer is: Beyond all question, in large measure, through Religion; under whose auspices so many great undertakings were set on foot, through whose aid they were brought to completion.

The present ills of society

A similar state of things would certainly have continued had the agreement of the two powers been lasting. More important results even might have been justly looked for, had obedience waited upon the authority, teaching, and counsels of the Church, and had this submission been specially marked by greater and more unswerving loyalty. For that should be regarded in the light of an ever-changeless law which Ivo of Chartres wrote to Pope Paschal II: " When kingdom and priesthood are at one, in complete accord, the world is well ruled, and the Church flourishes, and brings forth abundant fruit. But when they are at variance, not only smaller interests prosper not, but even things of greatest moment fall into deplorable decay " (*Epist. 238*).

Sad it is to call to mind how the harmful and lamentable rage for innovation which rose to a climax in the sixteenth century threw first of all into confusion the Christian religion, and next, by natural sequence, invaded the precincts of philosophy, whence it spread amongst all classes of society. From this source, as from a fountainhead, burst forth all those later tenets of unbridled license which, in the midst of the terrible upheavals of the last century, were wildly conceived and boldly proclaimed as the principles and foundation of that "new jurisprudence" which was not merely previously unknown, but was at variance on many points with not only the Christian, but even with the natural law.

Amongst these principles the main one lays down that as all men are alike by race and nature, so in like manner all are equal in the control of their life; that each one is so far his own master as to be in no sense under the rule of any other individual; that each is free to think on every subject just as he may choose, and to do whatever he may like to do; that no man has any right to rule over other men. In a society grounded upon such maxims, all government is nothing more nor less than the will of the people, and the people, being under the power of itself alone, is alone its own ruler. It does choose nevertheless some to whose charge it may commit itself, but in such wise that it makes over to them not the right so much as the business of governing, to be exercised, however, in its name. The authority of God is passed over in silence, just as if there were no God; or as if He cared nothing for human society; or as if men, whether in their individual capacity or bound together in social relations, owed nothing to God; or as if there could be a government of which the whole origin and power and authority did not reside in God Himself. Thus, as is evident, a State becomes nothing but a multitude, which is its own master and ruler. And since the populace is declared to contain within itself the springhead of all rights and of all power, it follows that the State does not consider itself bound by any kind of duty toward God. Moreover, it believes that it is not obliged to make public profession of any religion; or to inquire which of the very many religions is the only true one; or to prefer one religion to all the rest; or to show to any form of religion special favor; but, on the contrary, is bound to grant equal rights to every creed, so that public order may not be disturbed by any particular form of religious belief.

And it is a part of this theory that all questions that concern religion are to be referred to private judgment; that everyone is to be free to follow whatever religion he prefers, or none at all if he disapprove of all. From this the following consequences logically flow: that the judgment of each one's conscience is independent of all law; that the most unrestrained opinions may be openly expressed as to the practice or omission of Divine Worship; and that everyone has unbounded license to think whatever he chooses and to publish abroad whatever he thinks.

Now when the State rests on foundations like those just named — and for the time being they are greatly in favor — it readily appears into what and how unrightful a position the Church is driven. For when the management of public business is in harmony with doctrines of such a kind, the Catholic religion is allowed a standing in civil society equal only, or inferior, to societies alien from it; no regard is paid to the laws of the Church, and she who, by the order and commission of Jesus Christ, has the duty of teaching all nations, finds herself forbidden to take any part in the instruction of the people. With reference to matters that are of twofold jurisdiction, they who administer the civil power lay down the law at their own will, and in matters that appertain to religion, defiantly put aside the most sacred decrees of the Church. They claim jurisdiction over the marriages of Catholics, even over the bond as well as the unity and the indissolubility of matrimony.

They lay hands on the goods of the clergy, contending that the Church cannot possess property. Lastly, they treat the Church with such arrogance that, rejecting entirely her title to the nature and rights of a perfect society, they hold that she differs in no respect from other societies in the State, and for this reason possesses no right nor any legal power of action, save that which she holds by the concession and favor of the government. If in any State the Church retains her own right — and this with the approval of the civil law, owing to an agreement publicly entered into by the two powers — men forthwith begin to cry out that matters affecting the Church must be separated from those of the State.

Their object in uttering this cry is to be able to violate unpunished their plighted faith, and in all things to have unchecked control. And as the Church, unable to abandon her chiefest and most sacred duties, cannot patiently put up with this, and asks that the pledge given to her be fully and scrupulously acted up to, contentions frequently arise between the ecclesiastical and the civil power, of which the issue commonly is, that the weaker power yields to the one which is stronger in human resources.

Accordingly, it has become the practice and determination under this condition of public polity (now so much admired by many) either to forbid the action of the Church altogether, or to keep her in check and bondage to the State. Public enactments are in great measure framed with this design. The drawing up of laws, the administration of State affairs, the godless education of youth, the spoliation and suppression of religious orders, the overthrow of the temporal power of the Roman Pontiff, all alike aim at this one end — to paralyze the action of Christian institutions, to cramp to the utmost the freedom of the Catholic Church, and to curtail her every single prerogative.

Such concepts of government are wholly at variance with truth

Now, natural reason itself proves convincingly that such concepts of the government of a State are wholly at variance with the truth. Nature itself bears witness that all power, of every kind, has its origin from God, who is its chief and most august source.

The sovereignty of the people, however, and this without any reference to God, is held to reside in the multitude; which is doubtless a doctrine exceedingly well calculated to flatter and to inflame many passions, but which lacks all reasonable proof, and all power of insuring public safety and preserving order. Indeed from the prevalence of this teaching, things have come to such a pass that many hold as an axiom of civil jurisprudence that seditions may be rightfully fostered. For the opinion prevails that princes are nothing more than delegates chosen to carry out the will of the people; whence it necessarily follows that all things are as changeable as the will of the people, so that risk of public disturbance is ever hanging over our heads.

To hold, therefore, that there is no difference in matters of religion between forms that are unlike each other, and even contrary to each other, most clearly leads in the end to the rejection of all religion in both theory and practice. And this is the same thing as atheism, however it may differ from it in name. Men who really believe in the existence of God must, in order to be consistent with themselves and to avoid absurd conclusions, understand that differing modes of Divine Worship involving dissimilarity and conflict even on most important points, cannot all be equally probable, equally good, and equally acceptable to God.

So, too, the liberty of thinking, and of publishing, whatsoever each one likes, without any hindrance, is not in itself an advantage over which society can wisely rejoice. On the contrary, it is the fountainhead and origin of many evils. Liberty is a power perfecting man, and hence should have truth and goodness for its object. But the character of goodness and truth cannot be changed at option. These remain ever one and the same, and are no less unchangeable than Nature herself. If the mind assents to false opinions, and the will chooses and follows after what is wrong, neither can attain its native fullness, but both must fall from their native dignity into an abyss of corruption. Whatever, therefore, is opposed to virtue and truth, may not rightly be brought temptingly before the eye of man, much less sanctioned by the favor and protection of the law. A well-spent life is the only passport to heaven, whither all are bound, and on this account the State is acting against the laws and dictates of nature whenever it permits the license of opinion and of action to lead minds astray from truth, and souls away from the practice of virtue. To exclude the Church, founded by God Himself, from the business of life, from the power of making laws, from the training of youth, from domestic society, is a grave and fatal error. A State from which religion is banished can never be well regulated; and already perhaps more than is desirable is known of the nature and tendency of the so-called *civil* philosophy of life and morals. The Church of Christ is the true and sole teacher of virtue and guardian of morals. She it is who preserves in their purity the principles from which duties flow, and by setting forth most urgent reasons for virtuous life, bids us not only to turn away from wicked deeds, but even to curb all movements of the mind that are opposed to reason; even though they be not carried out in action.

To wish the Church to be subject to the civil power in the exercise of her duty is great folly and a sheer injustice. Whenever this is the case, order is disturbed, for things natural are put above things supernatural; the many benefits which the Church, if free to act, would confer on society are either prevented or at least lessened in number; and a way is prepared for enmities and contentions between the two powers; with how evil result to both the issue of events has taught us only too frequently.

Doctrines such as these, which cannot be approved by human reason, and most seriously affect the whole civil order, Our predecessors the Roman Pontiffs (well aware of what their apostolic office required of them) have never allowed to pass uncondemned. Thus Gregory XVI in his Encyclical Letter *Mirari vos*, of date August 15, 1832, inveighed with weighty words against the sophisms, which even at his time were being publicly inculcated — namely, that no preference should be shown for any particular form of worship; that it is right for individuals to form their own personal judgments about religion; that each man's conscience is his sole and all-sufficing guide; and that it is lawful for every man to publish his own views, whatever they may be, and even to conspire against the State. On the question of the separation of Church and State the same Pontiff writes as follows: "Nor can We hope for happier results either for religion or for the civil government from the wishes of those who desire that the Church be separated from the State, and the concord between the secular and ecclesiastical authority be dissolved. It is clear that these men, who yearn for a shameless liberty, live in dread of an agreement which has always been fraught with good, and advantageous alike to sacred and civil interests." To the like effect, also, as occasion presented itself, did Pius IX brand publicly many false opinions which were gaining ground, and afterward ordered them to be condensed in summary form in order that in this sea of error Catholics might have a light which they might safely follow. It will suffice to indicate a few of them:

Prop. xix. The Church is not a true, perfect, and wholly independent society, possessing its own unchanging rights conferred upon it by its Divine Founder; but it is for the civil power to determine what are the rights of the Church, and the limits within which it may use them.

Prop. xxix. The State, as the origin and source of all rights, enjoys a right that is unlimited.

Prop. lv. The Church must be separated from the State, and the State from the Church.

Prop. lxxix. . . . It is untrue that the civil liberty of every form of worship, and the full power given to all of openly and publicly manifesting whatsoever opinions and thoughts, lead to the more ready corruption of the minds and morals of the people, and to the spread of the plague of religious indifference.

From these pronouncements of the Popes it is evident that the origin of public power is to be sought for in God Himself, and not in the multitude, and that it is repugnant to reason to allow free scope to sedition. Again, that it is not lawful for the State, any more than for the individual, either to disregard all religious duties or to hold in equal favor different kinds of religion; that the unrestrained freedom of thinking and of openly making known one's thoughts is not inherent in the rights of citizens, and is by no means to be reckoned worthy of favor and support. In like manner it is to be understood that the Church no less than the State itself is a society perfect in its own nature and its own right, and that those who exercise sovereignty ought not so to act as to compel the Church to become subservient or subject to them, or to hamper her liberty in the management of her own affairs, or to despoil her in any way of the other privileges conferred upon her by Jesus Christ. In matters, however, of mixed jurisdiction, it is in the highest degree consonant to nature, as also to the designs of God, that so far from one of the powers separating itself from the other, or still less coming into conflict with it, complete harmony, such as is suited to the end for which each power exists, should be preserved between them.

This then is the teaching of the Catholic Church concerning the constitution and government of the State. By the words and decrees just cited, if judged dispassionately, no one of the several forms of government is in itself condemned, inasmuch as none of them contain anything contrary to Catholic doctrine, and all of them are capable, if wisely and justly managed, to insure the welfare of the State. Neither is it blameworthy in itself, in any manner, for the people to have a share, greater or less, in the government; for at certain times, and under certain laws, such participation may not only be of benefit to the citizens, but may even be of obligation. Nor is there any reason why anyone should accuse the Church of being wanting in gentleness of action or largeness of view, or of being opposed to real and lawful liberty. The Church, indeed, deems it unlawful to place the various forms of Divine Worship on the same footing as the true religion, but does not, on that account, condemn those rulers who, for the sake of securing some great good or of hindering some great evil, tolerate in practice that these various forms of religion have a place in the State. And in fact the Church is wont to take earnest heed that no one shall be forced to embrace the Catholic Faith against his will, for, as St. Augustine wisely reminds us, " Man cannot believe otherwise than of his own free will."

True and false liberty

In the same way the Church cannot approve of that liberty which begets a contempt of the most sacred laws of God, and casts off the obedience due to lawful authority, for this is not liberty so much as license, and is most correctly styled by St. Augustine the "liberty of self-ruin," and by the apostle St. Peter the "cloak of malice" (I Peter 2:16). Indeed, since it is opposed to reason, it is a true slavery, "for whosoever committeth sin is the slave of sin" (John 8:34). On the other hand, that liberty is truly genuine, and to be sought after, which in regard to the individual does not allow men to be the slaves of error and of passion, the worst of all masters; which, too, in public administration guides the citizens in wisdom and provides for them increased means of well-being; and which, further, protects the State from foreign interference.

This honorable liberty, alone worthy of human beings, the Church approves most highly and has never slackened her endeavor to preserve, strong and unchanged, among nations. And in truth whatever in the State is of chief avail for the common welfare; whatever has been usefully established to curb the license of rulers who are opposed to the true interests of the people, or to keep in check the leading authorities from unwarrantably interfering in municipal or family affairs; — whatever tends to uphold the honor, manhood, and equal rights of individual citizens; — of all these things, as the monuments of past ages bear witness, the Catholic Church has always been the originator, the promotor, or the guardian. Ever therefore consistent with itself, while on the one hand she rejects that exhorbitant liberty which in individuals and in nations ends in license or in thralldom, on the other hand, she willingly and most gladly welcomes whatever improvements the age brings forth, if these really secure the prosperity of life here below, which is as it were a stage in the journey to the life that will know no ending.

Therefore, when it is said that the Church is jealous of modern political systems, and that she repudiates the discoveries of modern research, the charge is a ridiculous and groundless calumny. Wild opinions she does repudiate, wicked and seditious projects she does condemn, and especially that habit of mind which points to the beginning of a willful departure from God. But as all truth must necessarily proceed from God, the Church recognizes in all truth that is reached by research, a trace of the divine intelligence. And as all truth in the natural order is powerless to destroy belief in the teachings of revelation, but can do much to confirm it, and as every newly discovered truth may serve to further the knowledge or the praise of God, it follows that whatsoever spreads the range of knowledge will always be willingly and even joyfully welcomed by the Church. She will always encourage and promote, as she does in other branches of knowledge, all study occupied with the investigation of nature. In these pursuits, should the human intellect discover anything not known before, the Church makes no opposition. She never objects to search being made for things that minister to the refinements and comforts of life. So far indeed from opposing these she is now as she ever has been, hostile alone to indolence and sloth, and earnestly wishes that the talents of men may bear more and more abundant fruit by cultivation and exercise. Moreover she gives encouragement to every kind of art and handicraft, and through her influence, directing all strivings after progress toward virtue and salvation, she labors to prevent man's intellect and industry from turning him away from God and from heavenly things.

All this, though so reasonable and full of counsel, finds little favor nowadays when States not only refuse to conform to the rules of Christian wisdom but seem even anxious to recede from them further and further on each successive day. Nevertheless, since truth when brought to light is wont, of its own nature, to spread itself far and wide, and gradually take possession of the minds of men, We, moved by the great and holy duty of Our Apostolic mission to all nations, speak, as We are bound to do, with freedom. Our eyes are not closed to the spirit of the times. We repudiate not the assured and useful improvements of our age, but devoutly wish affairs of State to take a safer course than they are now taking, and to rest on a more firm foundation without injury to the true freedom of the people. For the best parent and guardian of liberty amongst men is truth. " The truth shall make you free." (John 8:32.)

The duties of Catholics

If in the difficult times in which our lot is cast, Catholics will give ear to Us, as it behooves them to do, they will readily see what are the duties of each one in matters of opinion as well as action. As regards opinion, whatever the Roman Pontiffs have hitherto taught, or shall hereafter teach, must be held with a firm grasp of mind, and so often as occasion requires, must be openly professed.

Especially with reference to the so-called "Liberties" which are so greatly coveted in these days, all must stand by the judgment of the Apostolic See, and have the same mind. Let no man be deceived by the outward appearance of these *liberties*, but let each one reflect whence these have had their origin, and by what efforts they are everywhere upheld and promoted. Experience has made us well acquainted with their results to the State, since everywhere they have borne fruits which the good and wise bitterly deplore. If there really exist anywhere, or if we in imagination conceive, a State, waging wanton and tyrannical war against Christianity, and if we compare with it the modern form of government just described, this latter may seem the more endurable of the two. Yet, undoubtedly, the principles on which such a government is grounded are, as We have said, of a nature which no one can approve.

Secondly, action may relate to private and domestic matters, or to matters public. As to private affairs, the first duty is to conform life and conduct to the gospel precepts, and to refuse to shrink from this duty when Christian virtue demands some sacrifice difficult to make. All, moreover, are bound to love the Church as their common mother, to obey her laws, promote her honor, defend her rights, and to endeavor to make her respected and loved by those over whom they have authority. It is also of great moment to the public welfare to take a prudent part in the business of municipal administration, and to endeavor above all to introduce effectual measures, so that, as becomes a Christian people, public provision may be made for the instruction of youth in religion and true morality. Upon these things the well-being of every State greatly depends.

Furthermore, it is in general fitting and salutary that Catholics should extend their efforts beyond this restricted sphere, and give their attention to national politics. We say in general, because these Our precepts are addressed to all nations. However, it may in some places be true that, for most urgent and just reasons, it is by no means expedient for Catholics to engage in public affairs or to take an active part in politics. Nevertheless, as We have laid down, to take no share in public matters would be equally as wrong (We speak in general) as not to have concern for, or not to bestow labor upon, the common good. And this all the more because Catholics are admonished, by the very doctrines which they profess, to be upright and faithful in the discharge of duty; while if they hold aloof, men whose principles offer but small guarantee for the welfare of the State will the more readily seize the reins of government. This would tend also to the injury of the Christian religion, forasmuch as those would come into power who are badly disposed toward the Church, and those who are willing to befriend her would be deprived of all influence.

It follows therefore clearly that Catholics have just reasons for taking part in the conduct of public affairs. For in so doing they assume not the responsibility of approving what is blameworthy in the actual methods of government, but seek to turn these very methods, so far as is possible, to the genuine and true public good, and to use their best endeavors at the same time to infuse, as it were, into all the veins of the State the healthy sap and blood of Christian wisdom and virtue. The morals and ambitions of the heathens differed widely from those of the Gospel, yet Christians were to be seen living undefiled everywhere in the midst of pagan superstition, and, while always true to themselves, coming to the front boldly wherever an opening was presented. Models of loyalty to their rulers, submissive, so far as was permitted, to the sovereign power, they shed around them on every side a halo of sanctity; they strove to be helpful to their brethren, and to attract others to the wisdom of Jesus Christ, yet were bravely ready to withdraw from public life, nay, even to lay down their life, if they could not without loss of virtue retain honors, dignities, and offices. For this reason Christian ways and manners speedily found their way not only into private houses but into the camp, the Senate, and even into the imperial palaces. "We are but of yesterday," wrote Tertullian, "yet we swarm in all your institutions, we crowd your cities, islands, villages, towns, assemblies, the army itself, your wards and corporations, the palace, the Senate, and the law courts." So that the Christian faith, when once it became lawful to make public profession of the Gospel, appeared in most of the cities of Europe, not like an infant crying in its cradle, but already grown up and full of vigor.

In these our days it is well to revive these examples of our forefathers. First and foremost it is the duty of all Catholics worthy of the name and wishful to be known as most loving children of the Church, to reject without swerving whatever is inconsistent with so fair a title; to make use of popular institutions, so far as can honestly be done, for the advancement of truth and righteousness; to strive that liberty of action shall not transgress the bounds marked out by nature and the law of God; to endeavor to bring back all civil society to the pattern and form of Christianity which We have described. It is barely possible to lay down any fixed method by which such purposes are to be attained, because the means adopted must suit places and times widely differing from one another. Nevertheless, above all things, unity of aim must be preserved, and similarity must be sought after in all plans of action. Both these objects will be carried into effect without fail, if all will follow the guidance of the Apostolic See as their rule of life, and obey the bishops whom the Holy Ghost has placed "to rule the church of God" (Acts 20:28). The defense of Catholicism, indeed, necessarily demands that in the profession of doctrines taught by the Church all shall be of one mind and all steadfast in believing; and care must be taken never to connive, in any way, at false opinions, never to withstand them less strenuously than truth allows. In mere matters of opinion it is permissible to discuss things with moderation, with a desire of searching into the truth, without unjust suspicion or angry recriminations.

Hence, lest concord be broken by rash charges, let this be understood by all, that the integrity of Catholic Faith cannot

be reconciled with opinions verging on Naturalism or Rationalism, the essence of which is utterly to sterilize Christianity,
and to install in society the supremacy of man to the exclu-
sion of God. Further, it is unlawful to follow one line of conduct in private and another in public, respecting privately the
authority of the Church, but publicly rejecting it: for this
would amount to joining together good and evil, and to putting
man in conflict with himself; whereas he ought always to be
consistent, and never in the least point nor in any condition of
life to swerve from Christian virtue.

But in matters merely political, as for instance the best form
of government, and this or that system of administration, a
difference of opinion is lawful. Those, therefore, whose piety
is in other respects known, and whose minds are ready to
accept in all obedience the decrees of the Apostolic See, cannot in justice be accounted as bad men because they disagree
as to subjects We have mentioned; and still graver wrong will
be done them, if — as We have more than once perceived with
regret — they are accused of violating, or of wavering in, the
Catholic Faith.

Let this be well borne in mind by all who are in the habit
of publishing their opinions, and above all by journalists. In
the endeavor to secure interests of the highest order there is
no room for intestine strife or party rivalries; since all should
aim with one mind and purpose to make safe that which is the
common object of all — the maintenance of Religion and of the
State.

If, therefore, there have hitherto been dissensions, let them
henceforth be gladly buried in oblivion. If rash or injurious
acts have been committed, whoever may have been at fault,
let mutual charity make amends, and let the past be redeemed
by a special submission of all to the Apostolic See.

In this way Catholics will attain two most excellent results:
they will become helpers to the Church in preserving and
propagating Christian wisdom, and they will confer the greatest benefits on civil society, the safety of which is exceedingly
imperiled by evil teachings and bad passions.

This, Venerable Brethren, is what We have thought it Our
duty to expound to all nations of the Catholic world touching

the Christian constitution of States and the duties of individual citizens.

COMMENT AND EXPLICATION

Christ has dominion over all mankind, both individually and collectively

" Since Christ has received from the Father absolute dominion over all created things so that all are subject to His will, they err grievously who would take from the Christ-Man power over temporal things. . . . The dominion of the Redeemer embraces, therefore, all men, as was said in the words of Our Predecessor of lasting memory, Leo XIII, which We here gladly make our own: ' The Empire of Christ extends not only over Catholic peoples and over those who, reborn in the font of Baptism, belong by right to the Church, even though error has driven them far from her and dissension has separated them from the bond of love; it embraces even those who do not enjoy the privilege of the Christian Faith, so that all mankind must be said to be under the dominion of Jesus Christ ' (*Annum Sacrum*, May 25, 1899). Nor is any distinction to be made between individuals, the home, or civil society, for men are no less under the dominion of Christ when united in social groups than as single individuals." Pius XI, *Quas primas*, December 11, 1925.[3]

The significance of the Feast of Christ the King

" It is Our great pleasure to point out briefly what advantages for the Church, for society, and for each Christian We hope will flow from this public cult of Christ, King. In the first place, the very fact of our acknowledging publicly the royal honors which belong to Our Lord, must of itself recall that the Church which was established by

Him as a perfect society cannot but demand as her right, a right which she cannot renounce, full liberty and independence from the civil power. Moreover, the Church, in the exercise of her divine ministry of teaching, ruling, and guiding to eternal happiness all who belong to the Kingdom of Christ, manifestly cannot depend on the will of others. . . . The annual celebration of this feast will also become a means of recalling to the nations their duty of publicly worshiping Christ, that to render Him obedience is not only the duty of private individuals but of rulers and governments as well. It will recall that at the final judgment the Christ who has been ignored and despised, and even driven from public life and public affairs, will avenge all the injuries He has received. His royal dignity demands that society in general conform itself to the commandments of God and to the principles of the Christian life, first in the making of laws, then in the administration of justice, and above all things in preparing the souls of our young people for the acceptance of sound doctrine and the leading of holy lives." Pius XI, *Quas primas,* December 11, 1925.[4]

Government does not arise from the free consent of the governed

" Those who believe civil society to have arisen from the free consent of men, looking for the origin of its authority from the same source, say that each individual has given up something of his right, and that voluntarily every person has put himself into the power of that man in whose person the whole of those rights have been centered. But it is a great error not to see what is manifest, that men, as they are not a nomad race, have been created without their own free will for a natural community of life; and besides, that the agreement which they allege is openly a falsehood and a fiction and that it has no authority to confer on political power such great force, dignity, and firmness as the safety of the State and the common good of the citizens require." Leo XIII, *Diuturnum*, June 29, 1881.[5]

Sovereignty does not reside in the people

" Very many men of more recent times, walking in the footsteps of those who in former ages assumed to themselves the name of philosophers, say that all power comes from the people, so that those who exercise it in the State do so, not as their own, but as delegated to them by the people, and that, by this view, it can be revoked by the will of the very people by whom it was delegated. But from these [views] Catholics dissent, who affirm that the right to rule is from God as from a natural and necessary principle." Leo XIII, *Diuturnum*, June 29, 1881.[6]

Rulers may only be designated

" It is important to remark, in this place, that those who may be placed over the State may in certain cases be chosen by the will and decision of the multitude — without opposition to, or impugning of, the Catholic doctrine. And by this choice, in truth, the prince is designated, but the rights of princedom are not thereby conferred. Nor is this authority delegated to him, but the person by whom it is to be exercised is determined upon." Leo XIII, *Diuturnum*, June 29, 1881.[7]

Hierarchical structure of society ordained by God

" He who created and governs all things has, in his wise providence, appointed that the things which are lowest should attain their ends by those which are intermediate, and these again by the highest. Thus, as even in the kingdom of heaven he hath willed that the choirs of angels be distinct and some subject to others, and also in the Church has instituted various orders and a diversity of offices, . . . so also has he appointed that there should be various orders in civil society, differing in dignity, rights, and power, whereby the State, like the Church, should be one body, consisting of many members, some nobler than others, but all necessary to each other and solicitous for the common good." Leo XIII, *Quod Apostolici muneris,* December 28, 1878.[8]

The Condemnation of the Sillon

[The *Sillon* was a French political group that had grown out of a Catholic student movement in the 1890's. Animated by what it regarded as the true Christian spirit, it had become frankly democratic and republican in its political sympathies. In conformity with its democratic ideals, it resisted clerical control. The priests who joined were accepted simply as comrades, on the basis of equality.]

"We have long hesitated, venerable brethren, to express our thoughts on the *Sillon* publicly and solemnly. Your anxieties had to swell ours to decide Us to do so. . . . Counsels have not been wanting to them. Admonitions came after the counsels; but We have had the sorrow to see both advice and reproaches pass unnoticed and remain without result. Things came to this pitch that We should betray our duty if We kept silence any longer. . . . The *Sillon* puts forward as a program the elevation and regeneration of the working classes. But in this matter the principles of Catholic doctrine are fixed, and the history of Christian civilization attests their beneficent fruitfulness. Our predecessor of happy memory reminded them of this in masterly pages which Catholics occupied with social questions ought to study and keep always under their eyes. Notably he taught that Christian democracy ought ' to maintain the diversity of classes which is assuredly a fitting characteristic of a well-constituted State, and to wish for human society the form and character that God, its Author, impressed upon it.' He denounced ' a certain democracy which goes so far in perversity as to attribute in society sovereignty to the people and to aim at the suppression and the leveling down of the classes.' At the same time, Leo XIII laid down for Catholics a program of action, the only program capable of replacing and maintaining society on secular Christian bases. But what have the leaders of the *Sillon* done? Not only have they adopted a program and teaching different from that of Leo XIII (which would of itself be a singularly audacious movement on the part of laymen thus taking up concurrent with the Sovereign Pontiff the attitude of directors of social activity in the Church), but they have openly rejected the program traced by Leo XIII and have adopted one diametrically opposed to it; moreover, they reject the doctrine set forth by Leo XIII as to the essential principles of society, place the authority in the people, or gradually suppress it and strive, as their ideal, to realize the leveling down of the classes. In opposition to Catholic doctrine, therefore, they are proceeding toward a condemned ideal." Pius X, *Condemnation of the* Sillon, August 25, 1910.[9]

The Sillon *wishes each citizen to be a kind of king*

" In politics, the *Sillon* does not abolish authority; on the contrary it considers it necessary; but it wishes to divide it, or rather to multiply it, in such a way that each citizen will become a kind of king. Authority, it is true [according to their theory], emanates from God, but it resides first of all in the people and is obtained from them by means of election . . . without at the same time leaving the people and becoming independent of them." Pius X, *Condemnation of the* Sillon, August 25, 1910.[10]

The Sillon *holds the false view that power can ascend upward*

" The *Sillon* places public authority first of all in the people, from whom it then flows to rulers in such a manner, however, that it continues to reside in the people. But Leo XIII formally condemned this doctrine of political government in his encyclical ' *Diuturnum.*' . . . No doubt the *Sillon* holds that that authority, which it places first of all in the people, descends from God, but it holds that it descends in such a way ' as to return from below upwards, whilst in the organization of the Church power descends from above downwards.' But, besides it being abnormal for the delegation of power to ascend, since it is natural to it to descend, Leo XIII refuted in advance this attempt to reconcile Catholic doctrine with the error of philosophism. . . . For the rest, if the people are the holders of power, what becomes of authority? It is a shadow, a myth; there is no more law properly so called, no more obedience." Pius X, *Condemnation of the* Sillon, August 25, 1910.[11]

The Sillon *denies the hierarchical structure of society*
" The *Sillon* regards itself as the nucleus of the State of the future and accordingly reflects it as closely as possible. Thus, there is no hierarchy of government in the *Sillon*. The elite by whom it is directed emerge from the rank and file by selection, that is to say, they make their position

by their moral authority and other qualities. People enter its ranks freely and leave them freely. Studies are carried on without a master, at the very most with an adviser. The study clubs are veritable intellectual co-operative societies, in which each member is at once both master and pupil. . . . Even the priest, on entering, lowers the eminent dignity of his priesthood, and by a strange reversal of roles becomes a scholar, placing himself on a level with his young friends, so that he is no more than a comrade.

" In these democratic customs and the theories on the ideal State inspired by them, you will see, venerable brethren, the secret cause of the lack of discipline with which you have so often had to reproach the *Sillon*. It is not surprising that we do not find among the leaders or their members, whether seminarists or priests, trained on these lines, the respect, docility, and obedience which are due to your persons and authority." Pius X, *Condemnation of the* Sillon, August 25, 1910.[12]

The Sillon *believes in the efficacy of discussion*

" What must be thought of the promiscuousness in which young Catholics will be mixed up with heterodox and unbelieving folk of every kind in a work of this nature? . . . What must we think of this appeal to all the heterodox and to all the unbelievers to prove the excellence of their convictions in the social sphere in a sort of apologetic competition . . . ? What must we think of this respect for all errors and of the strange indication addressed by a Catholic to all dissidents to strengthen their convictions by study and to make them sources, more and more abundant, of new forces? What must we think of an association in which all religions and even free thought can manifest themselves openly and at their ease; for the

Sillonists, who at their public conferences and elsewhere proudly proclaim their individual faith, do not certainly know how to close the mouth of others and to prevent the Protestant from affirming his Protestantism and the skeptic from affirming his skepticism? . . . We fear that there is still worse. The result of this promiscuousness and labor, the beneficiary of this cosmopolitan social action, can only be a democracy which will be neither Catholic, nor Protestant, nor Jewish." Pius X, *Condemnation of the Sillon,* August 25, 1910.[13]

The authority of the church is not limited to persuasion
" Others do not oppose the existence of the Church . . . , yet they rob her of the nature and rights of a perfect society, and maintain that it does not belong to her to legislate, to judge, or to punish, but only to exhort, to advise, and to rule her subjects according to their own consent and will. By their opinion they would pervert the nature of this Divine society, and attenuate and narrow its authority. . . . To completely refute such teaching, the arguments . . . set forth by Us, especially in the encyclical letter *Immortale Dei* are of great avail; for by those arguments it is proved that, by a Divine provision, all the rights which essentially belong to a society that is legitimate, supreme, and perfect in all its parts exist in the Church." Leo XIII, *Libertas,* June 20, 1888.[14]

The authority of the church has precedence in matters of mixed jurisdiction
" The supernatural love for the Church and the natural love of our own country proceed from the same eternal principle, since God himself is their Author and originating Cause. Consequently it follows that between the duties they respectively enjoin, neither can come into collision

with the other. . . . The order of precedence of these
duties is, however, at times, either under stress of public
calamities, or through the perverse will of men, inverted.
For instances occur where the State seems to require from
men as subjects one thing, and religion from men as Christians quite another; and this in reality without any other
ground than that the rulers of the State either hold the
sacred power of the Church of no account, or endeavor
to subject it to their own will. Hence arises a conflict and
an occasion, through such conflict, of virtue being put to
the proof. . . . As to which should be preferred no one
ought to balance for an instant. It is a high crime indeed
to withdraw allegiance from God in order to please men;
an act of consummate wickedness to break the laws of
Jesus Christ in order to yield obedience to earthly rulers,
or, under pretext of keeping the civil law, to ignore the
rights of the Church." Leo XIII, *Sapientiae christianae,*
January 10, 1890.[15]

*Laws at variance with the teaching of the church are
invalid and need not be obeyed*

" If the laws of the State are manifestly at variance with
the divine law, containing enactments hurtful to the
Church, or conveying injunctions adverse to the duties
imposed by religion, or if they violate in the person of the
Supreme Pontiff the authority of Jesus Christ, then truly,
to resist becomes a positive duty, to obey, a crime; a crime,
moreover, combined with misdemeanor against the State
itself, inasmuch as every offense leveled against religion
is also a sin against the State. . . . Commands that are
issued adversely to the honor due to God, and hence are
beyond the scope of justice, must be looked upon as anything rather than laws." Leo XIII, *Sapientiae christianae,*
January 10, 1890.[16]

Any violation of the rights of God over civil society cannot be tolerated

" The Church does not desire . . . to mix up without just cause in the direction of purely civil affairs. On the other hand, she cannot permit or tolerate that the State use the pretext of certain laws or unjust regulations to do injury to the rights of an order superior to that of the State, to interfere with the constitution given the Church by Christ, or to violate the rights of God himself over civil society." Pius XI, *Ubi arcano*, December 23, 1922.[17]

The acts of a nation must conform to the teaching of the church

" The Church teaches (she alone has been given by God the mandate and the right to teach with authority) that not only our acts as individuals but also as groups and as nations must conform to the eternal law of God. In fact, it is much more important that the acts of a nation follow God's law, since on the nation rests a much greater responsibility for the consequences of its acts than on the individual." Pius XI, *Ubi arcano*, December 23, 1922.[18]

Separation of church and state, a most pernicious error

" That the State must be separated from the Church is a thesis absolutely false, a most pernicious error. Based, as it is, on the principle that the State must not recognize any religious cult, it is in the first place guilty of a great injustice to God; for the Creator of man is also the Founder of human societies, and preserves their existence as He preserves our own. We owe Him, therefore, not only a private cult, but a public and social worship to honor Him. Besides, it is an obvious negation of the supernatural order. It limits the action of the State to the pursuit of public prosperity during this life only, which is but the proximate object of political societies; and it occupies itself in no fashion (on the plea that this is foreign to it) with their ultimate object, which is man's eternal happiness after this short life shall have run its course. But as the present order of things is temporary and subordinated to the attainment of man's supreme and absolute welfare, it follows that the civil power must not only place no obstacle in the way of this object, but must aid us in effecting it. It also upsets the order providentially established by God in the world, which demands a harmonious agreement between the two societies, the civil and the religious, although each exercises its authority in its own sphere. . . . Finally, it inflicts great injury on society itself, for it cannot either prosper or last long when due place is not left for religion, which is the supreme rule and the sovereign mistress in all questions touching the rights and duties of men. Hence the Roman Pontiffs have never ceased, as circumstances required, to refute and condemn the doctrine of the separation of Church and State." Pius X, *Vehementer Nos*, February 11, 1906.[19]

Any education that neglects papal teaching is a crime against God

" Any training of the young which neglects, of deliberate purpose, to direct their minds toward a heavenly country . . . does a grave wrong to the souls of those who are concerned. . . . It has gone beyond the bounds of its own commission, and the situation is one which calls for a remedy in the interest of public welfare. Such secular education may seem to those, who take the responsibility for it, a source of hardihood and vigor; but the events which lie before us will prove the fallacy of such an estimate. Any training of young minds which neglects or repudiates the feeling and the spirit of the Christian religion is a crime of high treason against Him, who is ' King of

Kings and Lord of Lords.' " Pius XII, *Summi Pontificatus,* October 20, 1939.[20]

Freedom of religion condemned

" Let us examine that liberty in individuals which is so opposed to the virtue of religion, namely, the *liberty of worship,* as it is called, which rests on this principle, that every man is free to profess as he chooses any religion or none. But, assuredly, of all the duties which man has to fulfill, that, without doubt, is the chiefest and holiest which commands him to worship God with devotion and piety. . . . And, if it be asked, which of the many conflicting religions it is necessary to embrace, reason and the natural law unhesitatingly answer, that one which God commands, and which men can without difficulty recognize for themselves by certain exterior signs, whereby Divine Providence has willed that it should be distinguished, because, in a matter of such moment, the most terrible loss would be the consequence of any error. Wherefore, with a freedom such as We have described, to man is given the power to pervert or abandon with impunity the most sacred of duties, and to exchange the unchangeable good for evil; which, as We have said, is not liberty, but the degradation of liberty, and the abject surrender of the soul to sin. . . .

" Justice therefore forbids, and reason forbids, the State to be godless; or to adopt a line of action which would end in godlessness — namely, to treat the various religions (as they call them) alike, and to bestow upon them promiscuously equal rights and privileges." Leo XIII, *Libertas,* June 20, 1888.[21]

Freedom of speech and of the press condemned

" We must now consider a little the liberty of speech and the liberty of the press. It is hardly necessary to say that there can be no such right as this, if it be not used in moderation, and if it passes beyond the bounds and end of all true liberty. For right is a moral power which — as We have said and must again repeat — it is absurd to suppose that nature has accorded indifferently to truth and false-hood, to justice and injustice. Men have a right freely and prudently to propagate throughout the State whatsoever things are true and honorable, so that as many as possible may possesses them; but false doctrines, than which no mental plague is greater, and vices which corrupt the heart, should be diligently repressed by public authority, lest they insiduously work the ruin of the State. The ex-cesses of an unbridled intellect, which really end in the oppression of the ignorant multitude, are not less rightly restrained by the authority of the law than are the injuries inflicted by force upon the weak; and even more so, be-cause by far the greater part of the community either ab-solutely cannot, or can only with great difficulty, avoid their illusions and subtleties, especially such as flatter their own passions. If unbridled license of speech and writing be granted to all, nothing will remain sacred and inviolate." Leo XIII, *Libertas,* June 20, 1888.[22]

When error can be tolerated

" With the discernment of a true mother, the Church weighs the great burden of human weakness; and she knows what is the course in which the minds and affairs of men are now borne along. For this reason, while not conceding any right to anything that is not true and honest, it does not forbid public authority to tolerate what is at variance with truth and justice, for the sake of avoid-ing some greater evil, or of obtaining or preserving some greater good. . . . But to judge rightly, We must acknowledge that the more a State has to tolerate evil, the further is it from perfection; and that the tolerance of evil, which is suggested by political prudence, must be circumscribed by the limits which its cause, the public welfare, requires." Leo XIII, *Libertas,* June 20, 1888.[23]

In happier times the church would insist upon her own liberty

" Although in the extraordinary condition of these times the Church usually acquiesces in certain modern liberties, not because she prefers them in themselves, but because she judges it expedient to permit them, she would in happier times exercise her own liberty; and, by persuasion, exhortation, and entreaty, would endeavor, as she is bound, to fulfill the duty assigned to her by God of providing for the eternal salvation of mankind. One thing, however, remains always true — that the liberty which is claimed for all to do all things is not, as We have often said, of itself desirable, inasmuch as it is contrary to reason that error and truth should have equal rights." Leo XIII, *Libertas,* June 20, 1888.[24]

Only the Roman Pontiff may determine what concessions particular circumstances may require

" The rule of life which is laid down for Catholics is not of such a nature that it cannot accommodate itself to the exigencies of various times and places. The Church has, guided by her Divine Master, a kind and merciful spirit, for which reason from the very beginning she has been what St. Paul said of himself: ' I became all things to all men that I might save all.' History proves clearly that the Apostolic See, to which has been entrusted the mission not only of teaching but of governing the whole Church, has continued ' in one and the same doctrine, one and the same sense, and one and the same judgment ' (*Const. de fide,* c. iv.). But in regard to ways of living she has been accustomed to so yield that, the divine principle of morals being kept intact, she has never neglected to accommodate herself to the character and genius of the nations which she embraces. Who can doubt that she will act in the same spirit again if the salvation of souls requires it? In this matter the Church must be the judge, not private men who are often deceived by the appearance of right." Leo XIII, *Testem benevolentiae,* January 22, 1899.[25]

Instructions for Americans

" We highly esteem and love exceedingly the young and vigorous American nation, in which We plainly discern latent forces for the advancement alike of civilization and of Christianity. . . . That your Republic is progressing and developing by giant strides is patent to all; and this holds good in religious matters also. . . . The prosperous condition of Catholicity must be ascribed, first, indeed, to the virtue, the ability, and the prudence of the bishops and clergy; but in no slight measure also, to the faith and generosity of the Catholic laity. . . . But, moreover (a fact which it gives pleasure to acknowledge), thanks are due to the equity of the laws which obtain in America and to the customs of the well-ordered Republic. For the Church amongst you, unopposed by the Constitution and government of your nation, fettered by no hostile legislation, protected against violence by the common laws and the impartiality of the tribunals, is free to live and act without hindrance. Yet, though all this is true, it would be very erroneous to draw the conclusion that in America is to be sought the type of the most desirable status of the Church, or that it would be universally lawful or ex-

pedient for State and Church to be, as in America, dis-
severed and divorced. The fact that Catholicity with you is
in good condition, nay, is even enjoying a prosperous
growth, is by all means to be attributed to the fecundity
with which God has endowed his Church, in virtue of
which, unless men or circumstances interfere, she spontaneously expands and propagates herself; but she would
bring forth more abundant fruits if, in addition to liberty,
she enjoyed the favor of the laws and the patronage of the
public authority. . . .

" As regards civil affairs, experience has shown how important it is that the citizens should be upright and virtuous. . . . Let those of the clergy, therefore, who are occupied with the instruction of the multitude, treat plainly
this topic of the duties of ctiizens, so that all may understand and feel the necessity, in political life, of conscien-
tiousness, self-restraint, and integrity; for that cannot be
lawful in public which is unlawful in private affairs. On
this whole subject there are to be found, as you know, in
the encyclical letters written by Us from time to time in
the course of Our pontificate, many things which Catholics should attend to and observe. In these writings and
expositions We have treated of human liberty, of the chief
Christian duties, of civil government, and of the Christian
constitution of States, drawing Our principles as well from
the teaching of the Gospels as from reason. They, then,
who wish to be good citizens and discharge their duties
faithfully may readily learn from Our Letters the ideal of
an upright life." Leo XIII, *Longinqua oceani*, January 6,
1895.[26]

IV

CHRISTIAN DEMOCRACY

THE Roman Catholic Church, it is asserted again and again, is not bound to any one form of government, whether it be monarchy, aristocracy, or democracy. But the assertion that the church approves with impartiality all forms of government is always accompanied by a significant qualification. Pius XI (1922–1939) stated the qualification in these words: ". . . provided the divine rights of God and of Christian consciences are safe." [1] Leo XIII (1878–1903) put the qualification more fully: " It is not of itself wrong to prefer a democratic form of government, if only the Catholic doctrine be maintained as to the origin and use of power. Of the various forms of government, the Church does not reject any that are fitted to procure the welfare of the subjects; she wishes only — and this nature itself requires — that they should be constituted without wrong to any one, and especially without violating the rights of the Church." [2] This proviso, in reality, eliminates democracy as a theoretically permissible form of government, for it involves — as we have seen— a specific condemnation of almost every basic democratic doctrine.

On the other hand, the fact that democracy is not theoretically permissible does not mean that the Roman

Church cannot *adapt* itself to democratic societies, for quite obviously it has and does so adapt itself. ("Adapt," "adjust," and "reconcile" are always key words in any discussion of the relationship of Roman Catholic doctrine to democratic rights, and this is quite different from providing a positive foundation for a democratic society.) The basis on which this *adjustment* of Roman Catholic theory takes place, so that it may be *reconciled* with the principles of democracy, has been noted in the preceding chapter; namely, when due to particular circumstances and conditions the church judges it "expedient," for "the sake of avoiding some greater evil or of obtaining or preserving some greater good," to acquiesce in what is "at variance with truth and justice."[3] For the non-Catholic, who does not have the basic trust which the faithful are able to place in the Roman Pontiff, there is scant comfort to be found in this ability to adapt and reconcile, for to base democratic liberties only on the "fatherly indulgence" of the Bishop of Rome is to provide these liberties with what can only be regarded as a highly precarious foundation.

The ability to adjust and to reconcile its doctrine to the exigencies of a democratic society, however, was not the only apologetic adopted by the Roman Church. At a time when the tide of democratic sentiment was mounting and when the word "democracy" had gathered to itself such powerful emotional connotations that it was exerting — to use Toynbee's term — a widespread "charm" over the minds and hearts of many people, it seemed necessary to domesticate the word to Roman Catholic doctrine in such a way that, as occasion warranted, the Roman Church could profess its democratic sympathies boldly, eloquently, and affirmatively. This was accomplished by a verbal re-

definition of the word. A contrast was drawn between social democracy and Christian democracy. When the word
" democracy " was used in the latter sense, it was defined
as meaning " a benevolent and Christian movement in behalf of the people." So understood, democracy could mean
government *for* the people, but not necessarily *of* and *by*
the people. It was with this definition in mind that Leo
XIII was able to say, " If there is such a thing as a perfect
democratic form, this is undoubtedly to be found in the
Church." [4]

The use of the word " democracy " in a sense that
Leo XIII acknowledged was far removed from either its
" philological " or " philosophical " meaning has increased
the semantic difficulties experienced by the average reader
of papal documents. This is notably true of the discussion
of democracy by Pius XII in his Christmas Message of
1944, where a studied ambiguity combined with the problem of semantics makes the clear teaching of the church
unduly obscure.

If one is to understand what is meant by democracy in
this document, one must distinguish between those portions of the document in which Pius XII is speaking as a
reporter and those in which he is speaking as the teacher
of the faithful. At the outset, for example, he notes that
the peoples of the world " are more aggressive in opposing the concentration of dictatorial power " and that they
are " firmly convinced " that " had there been the possibility of censuring and correcting the actions of public
authority, the world would not have been dragged into the
vortex of a disastrous war." " In such a psychological atmosphere," he continues, " is it to be wondered at if the
tendency toward democracy is capturing the peoples and
winning a large measure of consent and support? " The

significant feature of this section is that Pius XII is only
reporting. He pronounces no judgment as to whether or
not this growing " conviction " of the people is valid.

It is important, in the second place, for the reader to
note the definitions that are given to several key words.
" Liberty," for example, means the " moral duty of the
individual." In keeping with this definition, the struggles
of the Roman Church to defend her special privileges and
prerogatives, at the expense of what might be considered
the " rights " of others, are to be regarded as " at the same
time struggles for man's true liberty." " Equality " means
" that, before the State, everyone has the right to live
honorably his own personal life in the place and under
the conditions in which the designs and dispositions of
Providence have placed him "; in other words, it means
an acceptance of the inequalities of social status that are
implicit in the God-given hierarchical structure of society.
" The dignity of man is the dignity of the moral community willed by God." " Absolutism," in this particular
document, does not refer either to an absolute monarchy
or to a fascist state. It refers to a democracy that exceeds
its powers and invades those realms which are beyond its
competence, one of the conspicuous characteristics of
absolutism being a disregard of the peculiar rights of the
Roman Church.

The third thing for the reader to observe is that the
document reveals a marked distrust of the untutored
" masses." The masses are " the capital enemy of true
democracy," and there is no sadder " spectacle " than that
of a state " left to the whims of the masses," nothing more
unfortunate than for the masses to be able to " impose its
whims on the better part of the real people." The " masses "
are to be distinguished from the " people "; and, since the

masses can only be directed and led, a true democracy is dependent upon men forming themselves into a " people "; a people that " lives and moves by its own life energy," which possesses " the true instinct for the common good," that is composed of men, " each of whom — at his proper place and in his own way — is a person conscious of his own responsibility and of his own views." By means of this distinction between the masses and the people, the hierarchical principle is introduced as an essential characteristic of true democracy.

A fourth thing for the reader to note is the apparent indifference of the document to the forms and structures of democratic government. Pius XII acknowledges that he is going to direct his attention to the problem of democracy and to examine " the forms by which it should be directed if it is to be a true, healthy democracy," but he never fulfills this promise. He immediately states that actually the interest of the church is not in the external structure and organization of democracy; it is in the kind of individuals the people must be who live under a democratic regime or who hold the reins of government in a democratic society. The forms are ostensibly a matter of relative indifference.

This apparent indifference may spring from an unwillingness to make too explicit the definition of the democracy that he is describing as permissible. In contradistinction to government by the masses, a true democracy seems to be " a people's government by honest and farseeing men." The implication would seem to be that a democracy may be little more than a government *for* the people, and throughout the document the question of how and by whom the rulers are to be selected or chosen seems to be studiously avoided. The " center of gravity " in a democracy, to be sure, is the popular assembly, the members of which are referred to as " the people's delegates." But are they to be elected by the masses or by the " people "? Or are these representatives of the people to be chosen and selected by an even smaller group? At this point the discussion becomes ambiguous, and it may be understood to mean that the legislative body may co-opt its own members. The legislative body, it is insisted, should " gather within it a group of select men "; a " select group " chosen from every profession and social grouping, " chosen for their solid Christian convictions, straight and steady judgment," who will remain " true to themselves in all circumstances "; men who will not look upon themselves as responsible to particular constituencies — " the mandatories of a mob whose interests are often unfortunately made to prevail over the true needs of the common good " — but who will so fulfill their obligations that they can " command the respect and support of the better section of the people." They are to be " men, above all, capable . . . to be leaders and heads, especially in times when the pressing needs of the moment excite the people's impressionability unduly and render it more liable to be led astray and get lost." They are to be, in brief, " guardians " of " the social order."

The teaching of this document may be summarized in terms of its insistence that " a sound democracy " must be " based on the immutable principles of the natural law and revealed truth," for they constitute " the ultimate foundation and directive norm of every democracy." But this, quite obviously, " is the fundamental criterion of every form of government." Two features alone, so far as the document is concerned, would seem to distinguish a democracy from other forms of government: the oppor-

tunity of an individual " to express his own views of the
duties and sacrifices that are imposed on him," and the
right not be be " compelled to obey without being heard."
Nothing is said as to whether or not he may continue to express his views, once they have been made known; and
nothing is said as to whether or not he shall have a share
in making the decision, for he may labor to make his views
prevail only " in a fashion conducive to the common
good." If he is only one of the " shapeless masses," he certainly is in no position to serve as a " guardian of the social
order " for whom " the natural law and revealed truth "
must be the criterion by which the " common good " is to
be judged.

In order to understand more fully the nature of " Christian democracy," we turn to the relevant portions of three
papal documents.

Encyclical Letter of Leo XIII, January 18, 1901
on
CHRISTIAN DEMOCRACY [5]

. . . Many excellent men find the term *Christian Democracy*
objectionable. They hold it to be very ambiguous, and for
this reason open to two objections. It seems by implication to
covertly favor popular government, and to disparage other
methods of political administration. Secondly, it appears to
belittle religion by restricting its scope to the care of the poor,
as if the other sections of Society were not of its concern.
More than that, under the shadow of its name there might
easily lurk a design to attack all legitimate power, either civil
or sacred. Wherefore, since this discussion is now so widespread, so exaggerated, and so bitter, the consciousness of
duty warns us to put a check on this controversy and to define what Catholics are to think on this matter. We also propose to describe how the movement may extend its scope and
be made more useful to the Commonwealth.

What *Social Democracy* is and what *Christian Democracy* ought to be, assuredly no one can doubt. The first, with due consideration to the greater or less intemperance of its utterance, is carried to such an excess by many as to maintain that there is really nothing existing above the natural order of things, and that the acquirement and enjoyment of corporal and external goods constitutes man's happiness. It aims at putting all government in the hands of the people, reducing all ranks to the same level, abolishing all distinction of class, and finally introducing community of goods. Hence, the right of ownership is to be abrogated, and whatever property a man possesses, or whatever means of livelihood he has, is to be common to all.

As against this, *Christian Democracy*, by the fact that it is Christian, is built, and necessarily so, on the basic principles of Divine Faith, and provides for the betterment of the masses, with the ulterior object of availing itself of the occasion to fashion their minds for things which are everlasting. Hence, for *Christian Democracy* justice is sacred; it must maintain that the right of acquiring and possessing property cannot be impugned, and it must safeguard the various distinctions and degrees which are indispensable in every well-ordered Commonwealth. Finally it must endeavor to preserve in every human society the form and character which God ever impresses upon it. It is clear, therefore, that there is nothing in common between *Social* and *Christian Democracy*. They differ from each other as much as the sect of Socialism differs from the profession of Christianity.

Moreover, it would be a crime to distort this name of *Christian Democracy* to politics, for although democracy, both in its philological and philosophical significations, implies popular government, yet in its present application it is to be employed that, removing from it all political significance, it is to mean nothing else than a benevolent and Christian movement in behalf of the people. . . .

Let there be no question of fostering under this name of *Christian Democracy* any intention of diminishing the spirit of obedience, or of withdrawing people from their lawful rulers. . . .

Papal Allocution of Leo XIII, December 23, 1902
on

CHRISTIAN DEMOCRACY [6]

. . . Understood as the Church understands it, the democratic concept not only accords marvelously with the dictates of revelation and religious belief, but has even been born of Christianity and educated by it, and it is by the preaching of the Gospel that the nations have received it. Athens and Rome knew it not, before they heard the Divine Voice which said to men, "You are all brothers, and of one Father who is in heaven."

Outside of this democracy, which is called and which is Christian, there is a seditious and Godless democracy, which pursues other ideals and walks by other ways; and bitter are the days which it is preparing for the States which hatch it in their bosoms and caress it. . . .

Christmas Message of Pius XII, December 24, 1944
on

DEMOCRACY AND PEACE [7]

. . . Beneath the sinister lightning of the war that encompasses them, in the blazing heat of the furnace that imprisons them, the peoples have, as it were, awakened from a long torpor. They have assumed, in relation to the state and those who govern, a new attitude — one that questions, criticizes, distrusts.

Taught by bitter experience, they are more aggressive in opposing the concentration of dictatorial power that cannot be censured or touched, and call for a system of government more in keeping with the dignity and liberty of the citizens. These multitudes, uneasy, stirred by the war to their innermost depths, are today firmly convinced — at first perhaps in a vague and confused way but already unyieldingly — that had there been the possibility of censuring and correcting the actions of public authority, the world would not have been dragged into the vortex of a disastrous war, and that to avoid for the future the repetition of such a catastrophe we must vest efficient guarantees in the people itself.

In such a psychological atmosphere, is it to be wondered at if the tendency toward democracy is capturing the peoples and winning a large measure of consent and support from those who hope to play a more efficient part in the destinies of individuals and of society?

It is scarcely necessary to recall that, according to the teaching of the Church, " it is not forbidden to prefer temperate, popular forms of government, without prejudice, however, to Catholic teaching on the origin and use of authority," and that " the Church does not disapprove of any of the various forms of government, provided they be per se capable of securing the good of the citizens " (Leo XIII, Encyclical, *Libertas,* June 20, 1888).

If, then, on this feast day which commemorates both the benignity of the Incarnate Word and the dignity of man (both in its personal and social aspects), We direct Our attention to the problem of democracy, examining the forms by which it should be directed if it is to be a true, healthy democracy answering the needs of the moment, Our action shows clearly that the interest and solicitude of the Church looks not so much to its external structure and organization — which depend on the special aspirations of each people — as to the individual himself, who, so far from being the object and, as it were, a merely passive element in the social order, is, in fact, and must be and continue to be, its subject, its foundation, and its end.

Given that democracy, taken in the broad sense, admits of various forms, and can be realized in monarchies as well as in republics, two questions come up for Our consideration: First, what characteristics should distinguish the men who live under democracy and a democratic regime? Second, what characterization should distinguish the men who hold the reins of government in a democracy?

Characteristics proper to citizens in a democratic regime

To express his own views of the duties and sacrifices that are imposed on him; not compelled to obey without being heard; these are two rights of the citizen which find in democracy, as its name implies, their expression. From the solidity, harmony, and good results produced by this between the citizens and the Government, one may decide which democracy is really healthy and well balanced, and what is its life energy and power of expansion. If, then, we consider the extent and nature of the sacrifices demanded of all the citizens, especially in our day when the activity of the State is so vast and decisive, the democratic form of government appears to many as a postulate of nature, imposed by reason itself. When, however, people call for "democracy and better democracy," such a demand cannot have any other meaning than to place the citizen ever more in the position to hold his own personal opinion, to express it, and to make it prevail in a fashion conducive to the common good.

Hence follows a first conclusion with its practical consequence. The State does not contain in itself and does not mechanically bring together in a given territory a shapeless mass of individuals. It is and should in practice be the organic and organizing unity of a real people. The people and a shapeless multitude (or as it is called "the masses") are two distinct concepts.

The people lives and moves by its own life energy; the masses are inert of themselves and can only be moved from outside. The people lives by the fullness of life in the men that compose it, each of whom — at his proper place and in his own way — is a person conscious of his own responsibility and of his own views. The masses, on the contrary, wait for the impulse from outside, an easy plaything in the hands of anyone who exploits their instincts and impressions, ready to follow, in turn, today this flag, tomorrow another. From the exuberant life of a true people, an abundant rich life is diffused in the State and all its organs, instilling into them, with a vigor that is always renewing itself, the consciousness of their own responsibility, the true instinct for the common good.

The elementary power of the masses, deftly managed and employed, the State also can utilize. In the ambitious hands of one or several who have been artificially brought together for selfish aims, the State itself, with support of the masses, reduced to the minimum status of a mere machine, can impose its whims on the better part of the real people. The common interest remains seriously and for a long time injured by this process, and the injury is very often hard to heal.

Hence follows clearly another conclusion: the masses — as we have just defined them — are the capital enemy of true democracy and of its ideal of liberty and equality.

In a people worthy of the name, the citizen feels within him the consciousness of his personality, of his duties and rights, of his own freedom joined to respect for the freedom and dignity of others. In a people worthy of the name, all inequalities based not on whim but on the nature of things, inequalities of culture, possessions, social standing — without, of course, prejudice to justice and mutual charity — do not constitute any obstacle to the existence and the prevalence of a true spirit of union and brotherhood. On the contrary, so far from impairing civil equality in any way, they give it its true meaning; namely, that, before the State, everyone has the right to live honorably his own personal life in the place and under the conditions in which the designs and dispositions of Providence have placed him.

As against this picture of the democratic ideal of liberty and equality in a people's government by honest and farseeing men, what a spectacle is that of a democratic State left to the whims of the masses. Liberty, from being a moral duty of the individual, becomes a tyrannous claim to give free rein to a man's impulses and appetites to the detriment of others. Equality degenerates to a mechanical level, a colorless uniformity. The sense of true honor, of personal activity, of respect for tradition, of dignity — in a word all that gives life its worth — gradually fades away and disappears. And the only survivors are, on the one hand, the victims, deluded by the specious mirage of democracy naïvely taken for the genuine spirit of democracy with its liberty and equality; and, on the other, the more or less numerous exploiters who have known how to use the power of money and of organization in order to secure a privileged position above the others, and have gained power.

Characteristics of men holding power in a democratic state

The democratic State, whether it be monarchical or republican, should like any other form of government be entrusted with the power to command with real and effective authority.

The absolute order itself of beings and purposes — which shows that man is an independent person, namely, the subject of inviolable duties and rights, who is the source and end of his own social life — comprises the State also as a necessary society endowed with authority, without which it could neither exist nor live. And if men, using their personal liberty, were to deny all dependence on a superior authority possessing coercive power, they could by this very fact cut the ground from under their own dignity and liberty, by violating, that is, the absolute order of beings and purposes.

As they are established on this same foundation, the person, the State, the Government, with their respective rights, are so bound together that they stand or fall together. And since that absolute order — in the light of right reason, and in particular of the Christian faith — cannot have any other origin than in a personal God, our Creator, it follows that the dignity of man is the dignity of the moral community willed by God; the dignity of political authority is the dignity deriving from its sharing in the authority of God.

No form of State can avoid taking cognizance of this intimate and indissoluble connection — least of all a democracy. Accordingly, if those in power do not see it, or more or less discount it, their own authority is shaken; and social morality and that specious appearance of a purely formal democracy may often serve as a mark for all that is in reality least democratic. Only a clear appreciation of the purposes assigned by God to every human society, joined to a deep sense of the exalted duties of social activity, can put those in power in a position to fulfill their own obligations in the legislative, judicial, and executive order with that objectivity, impartiality, loyalty, generosity, and integrity, without which a democratic government would find it hard to command the respect and the support of the better section of the people.

The deep sense of the principles underlying a political and social order that is sound and conforms to the norms of right and justice is of special importance in those who in any kind of a democratic regime have, as the people's delegates, in whole or part, the power to legislate. And since the center of gravity of a democracy normally set up resides in this popular assembly from which political currents radiate into every field of public life — for good or ill — the question of the high moral standards, practical ability, and intellectual capacity of parliamentary deputies is for every people living under a democratic regime a question of life and death, of prosperity and decadence, of soundness or perpetual unrest.

To secure effective action, to win esteem and trust, every legislative body should — as experience shows beyond doubt — gather within it a group of select men, spiritually eminent and of strong character, who shall look upon themselves as the representatives of the entire people and not the mandatories of a mob whose interests are often unfortunately made to prevail over the true needs of the common good — a select group of men not restricted to any profession or social standing but reflecting every phase of the people's life; men chosen for their solid Christian convictions, straight and steady judgment, with a sense of the practical and equitable, true to themselves in all circumstances; men of clear and sound principles, with sound and clear-cut proposals to make; men, above all, capable, in virtue of the authority that emanates from their untarnished consciences and radiates widely from them, to be leaders and heads, especially in times when the pressing needs of the moment excite the people's impressionability unduly and render it more liable to be led astray and get lost; men who in periods of transition — generally stormy and disturbed by passion, by divergent opinions, and opposing programs — feel themselves doubly under the obligation to send circulating through the veins of the people and of the State, burning with a thousand fevers, the spiritual antidote of clear views, kindly interest, a justice equally sympathetic to all, and a bias toward national unity and concord in a sincere spirit of brotherhood.

Peoples whose spiritual and moral temperament is sufficiently sound and fecund find it themselves and can produce the heralds and implements of democracy who live in such dispositions and know how effectively to put them into prac-

tice. But where such men are lacking, others come to take
their places in order to make politics serve their ambition and
be a quick road to profit for themselves, their caste, and their
class; while the race after private interests makes them lose
sight of completely and jeopardize the true common good.

A sound democracy, based on the immutable principles of
the natural law and revealed truth, will resolutely turn its back
on such corruption as gives to the State Legislature an unchecked and unlimited power, and moreover makes of the
democratic regime, notwithstanding an outward show to the
contrary, purely and simply a form of absolutism. State absolutism (not to be confused, as such, with absolute monarchy,
of which we are not treating here) consists in fact in the false
principle that the authority of the State is unlimited and that
in face of it — even when it gives free rein to its despotic aims,
going beyond the confines between good and evil — to appeal
to a higher law obliging in conscience is not admitted.

A man penetrated with right ideas about the State and authority and the power that he wields as guardian of social
order will never think of derogating the majesty of the positive law within the ambit of its natural competence. But this
majesty of positive law is only inviolable when it conforms —
or at least is not opposed — to the absolute order set up by
the Creator and placed in a new light by the revelation of the
Gospel. It cannot subsist except in so far as it respects the
foundations on which human personality rests, no less than
the State and the Government. This is the fundamental criterion of every form of government, including democracy. It is
the criterion by which the moral value of every particular law
should be judged. . . .

The church as the guardian of man's true dignity and liberty

At a time when the peoples find themselves with duties such
as perhaps they have never met before in the course of their
history, they feel deeply in their tortured hearts the desire,
impatient and almost instinctive, to take the reins of their
destiny in their own hands with more independence than
heretofore, hoping that thus they will find it easier to defend
themselves from the periodic invasions of violence which, like

a boiling lava torrent, spares nothing of all that they hold
sacred and dear.

Thank God, one may believe the time has passed when the
call to moral and gospel principles to guide the life of States
and peoples was disdainfully thrust aside as unreal. The events
of these war years have given ample evidence to confute, in a
harder way than one could ever have imagined, those who
spread such doctrines. The disdain they have affected toward
this supposed unreality has been changed into stark reality:
brutality, iniquity, destruction, annihilation.

If the future is to belong to democracy, an essential part in
its achievement will have to belong to the religion of Christ
and to the Church, the messenger of Our Redeemer's word
which is to continue His mission of saving men. For she
teaches and defends supernatural truths and communicates
the supernatural helps of grace in order to actuate the divinely
established order of beings and ends which is the ultimate
foundation and directive norm of every democracy. By her
very existence, the Church rises before the world as a shining
beacon to remind it constantly of that divine order. Her history reflects clearly her providential mission. The struggles,
which, coerced by the abuse of power, she has had to sustain
in defense of the liberty given her by God, were at the same
time struggles for man's true liberty.

The Church has the mission to announce to the world, which
is looking for better and more perfect forms of democracy,
the highest and most needed message that there can be: the
dignity of man, the call to be sons of God. It is the powerful
cry, which from the manger in Bethlehem to the furthest confines of the earth resounds in the ears of men at a time when
that dignity is tragically low. The holy story of Christmas pro-
claims this inviolable dignity of man with a vigor and authority
that cannot be gainsaid — an authority and vigor that in-
finitely transcends that which all possible declarations of the
rights of man could achieve. . . .

V

CATHOLIC ACTION

CATHOLIC ACTION may be loosely defined as organized lay activity on behalf of the Roman Catholic faith, and it is therefore a part of the general apostolate of the laity. There is a technical distinction between Catholic Action and other religious associations in which the laity participate. But, since the functions of the two types of organization overlap, the distinction has been confusing and the technical terminology has tended to break down. At the present time, the whole question of the proper terminology to be employed is being restudied by the Holy See and a new organizational structure may be proposed to correlate more closely the two types of organization (*Catholic Mind,* January–February, 1958, p. 81). The distinctions are somewhat complex and essentially irrelevant to our concern. To avoid confusion and ambiguity, the tendency of recent papal statements has been to minimize the technical distinction and to speak in terms of the lay apostolate in general. It may be of interest to note, however, that in the United States the directive body of Catholic Action is the National Catholic Welfare Conference.

Catholic Action had its origin in the situation created by the rise of democratic governments. In a democratic society issues that arose between church and state could no longer be resolved through direct negotiation with the prince, for public policy was determined by the people and not by the prince. In a democracy it is the people, through their elected parliamentary or legislative representatives, who are entrusted with the power to make decisions of greatest moment in the shaping of the common life, including the recognition or nonrecognition of the rights and privileges of the church. The people are free to debate and to enact laws concerning marriage, the family, the child, the school, and the church. They formulate the basic laws of both the political and economic order. Under these conditions, it was obvious that if the rights of the church — which were under severe attack — were to be preserved, and if the Christian order of society — which in many lands from the Roman Catholic point of view had been badly disfigured or destroyed — was to be restored, it could only be accomplished by the action of the faithful. As Pius XII more recently pointed out, " the relations between the Church and the world require the intervention of lay apostles." For, he continued, in a democratic society " the consecration of the world is essentially " and inevitably " the work of laymen themselves, of men who are intimately a part of economic and social life and who participate in the government and legislative assemblies." [1]

Although Pius IX (1846–1878) is known as the first " Catholic Action " Pope, and although Leo XIII (1878–1903) filled in and elaborated the major features of its mandate, it was Pius X (1903–1914) who perfected and systematized its organization during the first years of the twentieth century. At the beginning of his pontificate in 1903, Pius X announced that the goal of his endeavor was to be " the restoration of all things in Christ," and he insisted that this must also be the goal of Catholic Action. " The duty that has been imposed alike upon Us and upon you," he had written to the members of the hierarchy, is that "of bringing back to the discipline of the Church human society now estranged from the wisdom of Christ; the Church will then subject it to Christ, and Christ to God." But this task, he asserted, cannot be accomplished by the hierarchy and the priesthood alone. Due to "the present condition of the Church and society," it requires the active co-operation of the laity. Thus "all the faithful" must be actively enlisted in a concern for "the interests of God" in the life of the world, dedicating themselves "to defend, to support, with a truly Catholic spirit, the rights of God in all things, and those, not less sacred, of the Church." [2]

A major concern of Pius X, in the nineteen rules of the *motu proprio* [3] that he formulated to govern the activities of Catholic Action, was to make it clear that Catholic Action must be subordinated to the control and direction of the hierarchy. In the Roman Catholic Church, the laity has no apostolate of its own. The only apostolate is the apostolate of the hierarchy. It was to the apostles that the Great Commission of Matt. 28:19–20 was addressed, and it was to the apostles that Christ said, " As my Father hath sent me, even so send I you " (John 20:21). From this commission to the apostles is derived the exclusive mandate and powers of the hierarchy. Thus the laity, having received no commission and possessing no powers from the apostles, are not capable of an independent apostolate. They may only assist or share in the apostolate of the hierarchy; and it is constantly emphasized that this assistance must be rendered in due subordination and obedience to the constituted authority of the church. What is commonly regarded as the classical definition of Catholic Action was formulated by Pius XI as follows: " The partici- pation of the Catholic Laity in the Hierarchic Apostolate, for the defense of religious and moral principles, for the development of a wholesome and beneficient social action, under the guidance of the ecclesiastical hierarchy, outside and above political parties, with the intention of restoring Catholic life in family and society." [4] More recently the tendency has been to substitute the word " collaboration " for " participation " in an endeavor to avoid any sugges- tion that the laity may possess of themselves any portion of the apostolate. They are only to " collaborate " — to help, to assist, to " become as it were the echo of the voice of their Masters." [5]

What, then, is the role of Catholic Action? It is to serve as an " auxiliary " to the hierarchy, to serve as " the lay militia " of the governing authority in its effort to restore human society to the discipline of the church.

The first work of Catholic Action is the " formation," within each of its members, of a Christian conscience with regard to the manifold issues that affect the life of the in- dividual, the family, the state, and the church. This is the first and great task, and it is indispensable to every other aim of Catholic Action.

If the immediate task of Catholic Action is the formation of the consciences of its own members and if its ultimate task is the reshaping of society to conform to papal teach- ing, it is clear that numerous instrumental activities must intervene. For one thing, if its ultimate goal is to be achieved, the " formative " work of Catholic Action must be extended to include the whole population. This means that Catholic Action must engage in instructing those within the church, in reclaiming those who have become indifferent, in evangelizing those who are outside, in strengthening "Christian" family life, and in diffusing "Christian" culture generally. It means that Catholic Action must engage in educational activity — both formal and informal — and that it must give special attention to the press and other mass media of communication by which the mind of both individuals and society is shaped. It means, moreover, that Catholic Action must engage in humanitarian activity to relieve distress, and that its members must participate in labor and other similar organizations in an effort to counter "anti-Christian" tendencies and to win support for the "Christian" solution to the social problem.

While Catholic Action itself may not engage in "politics" as a political party, being "outside and above political parties," it is profoundly concerned with political affairs. Its members, as individuals, should engage in political activities, and, if it seems wise, they may form a Catholic political party. But Catholic Action itself, except when specific rights of the church are involved, is restricted to the shaping of the "Christian" conscience so that it may make itself felt in the voting booth, the ballot box, and the legislative assembly. As Pius XI put it, "When consciences shall have been Christian-wise formed, equipped, and instructed, the rest will come of itself."[6]

A comprehensive discussion of the nature, scope, and activities of Catholic Action is contained in the following three addresses by Pius XII.

Address of Pius XII, May 5, 1951
on

CATHOLIC ACTION [7]

. . . Our wish is to draw your attention to some considerations concerning Catholic Action in itself.

1. In the first place, you are " Catholic Action." This word
" Action," precise and comprehensive at the same time, indi-
cates the special character of your organization and distinguishes it from other Catholic associations. Not that the
latter do not also take action, but their activities are usually
geared toward a special, determined object carried out by
means of an organized and permanent society. . . . For this
reason, such bodies generally take their titles from their aim.

But you call yourselves simply " Catholic Action " because,
having a general, not particular or specific, aim, you are not,
as it were, a fixed axis around which gravitates the mechanism
of just any organization. You are rather a reception center
where Catholics gather to organize for action.

Given this, there cannot be among you (as there exist in
other associations in accordance with their rules and for a
useful purpose) side by side with the true and proper active
members, other " honorary " members who do nothing more
than subscribe to the objectives and aim of the association,
renew their membership regularly, pay their dues, and perhaps even subscribe to the periodical publications and attend
meetings from time to time. . . . Would a little nucleus of
active members accompanied by a shapeless crowd of adherents during the great public manifestations merit the name
of Catholic Action?

2. Catholic Action is by special title — and well you know
it — directly subordinated to the authority of the Hierarchy
and it collaborates with the latter in the apostolate. In Italian
Catholic Action, the headquarters and the various diocesan
and parochial groups are managed by the laity who, however,
are helped and guided by the assistance of the clergy. But in
the Marian Congregations (Sodalities of Our Lady), which
can also be called in the fullest sense of the term Catholic
Action, the parish priest is president by right. . . .

These thoughts on the organization of Catholic Action lead
Us to add some considerations of a general nature demanded
also by incorrect tendencies of our day.

In the first place, a word about the idea of the apostolate.
The apostolate does not consist merely in announcing the Good
News but also in leading men to the sources of salvation, at
the same time fully respecting their freedom, in converting

them and in training with ardent zeal those who are baptized
to become perfect Christians.

It would be a mistake to see in Catholic Action — as some
people have recently stated — something essentially new, a
change in the structure of the Church, a new apostolate of
laymen side by side with that of the priests and not subordinated to the latter. In the Church laymen have always collab-
orated in the apostolate of the Hierarchy in subordination to
the Bishop and to him to whom the Bishop has entrusted responsibility for the care of souls under his authority. Catholic
Action has given this collaboration nothing but a new form
of organization so that it may be better and more efficaciously
exercised. . . .

3. The activities of Catholic Action extend to the entire religious and social field covered by the mission and work of the
Church. It is well known that the normal growth and increase
of religious life presuppose a certain measure of healthy economic and social conditions. . . . But from this it cannot be
concluded that the Church must begin by laying aside its
religious mission and, first and foremost, procure the healing of
social misery. The Church has always been solicitous in the
defense and promotion of justice, but from the days of the
Apostles, even when faced with the gravest social abuses, she
has fulfilled her mission; and by the sanctification of souls and
the conversion of inner feelings, she has also sought to start the
cure of social evils — persuaded as she is that the power of
religion and Christian principles bring about this cure better
than any other means.

4. The external and well-disciplined organization of Catholic Action does not exclude, but even promotes, individual
perspicacity and a spirit of foresight and initiative — everyone
according to his own capacity and station — in permanent contact with the members of Catholic Action in the same place,
of the same profession, and of the same circle. Whenever the
need is felt for some Catholic action or campaign, each man
holds himself ready with a good heart. By his enthusiasm and
devotion, each brings disinterested help to other organizations
and institutions desirous of his collaboration in order to obtain
their own objective with greater security and perfection. . . .

5. We have no need to tell you that Catholic Action is not called upon to be a power in the field of party politics. Catholic citizens as such can well unite themselves in an association for political activity: they have every right to do this no less as Christians than as citizens. . . .

6. By its nature, Catholic Action has no mission to lead other associations or to exercise over them a semiauthoritative patronage. The fact that Catholic Action is under the immediate direction of the Hierarchy does not lead to such a conclusion. The special end of each organization is that which determines the manner of its direction. And it may well be that this end does not need, or even renders inopportune, such immediate direction. Yet this does not mean that these organizations cease to be Catholic and united to the Hierarchy. . . .

This leads to a conclusion which is at the same time a paternal warning — not for Catholic Action in any given country but for Catholic Action of all countries and of all times. The structure of Catholic Action must adapt itself in different regions to particular local circumstances. But in one point all its members are on the same footing: in thinking with the Church, in dedicating themselves to the Church's cause, in obeying those whom the Holy Ghost has made Bishops to rule the Church of God, in submitting as sons to the Supreme Pastor to whose care Christ has entrusted His Church. And how could it be otherwise as long as you, members of Catholic Action, together with your Bishop and your Pope, form, so to speak, virtually a single unit.

With this wish We wholeheartedly impart to you, beloved sons and daughters, Our Apostolic Benediction.

Address of Pius XII, October 14, 1951
on

The Lay Apostolate [8]

What consolation and joy overflow Our heart at the sight of this imposing assembly . . . , come together from all continents and regions to the center of the Church, to celebrate here this World Congress of the Lay Apostolate. . . . You have come to renew the expression of your faith, of your devotion, and of your fidelity to the Vicar of Jesus Christ, and to beg Him to make fruitful by His blessing your resolutions and activity. . . .

Frequently, indeed, in the course of Our Pontificate, We have spoken of this apostolate of the laity under the most diverse circumstances. . . . This time . . . , We would wish, in a very brief word to define its place and its role today in the light of the past history of the Church. Since from this history the lay apostolate has never been absent, it will be interesting and instructive to follow its development over the years.

The origin of Catholic Action

It is often said that during the past four centuries the Church has been exclusively " clerical " as a reaction against the movement which, in the sixteenth century, tried to achieve the abolition, pure and simple, of the hierarchy. . . . Such a judgment is so far from the reality that it is precisely following the sacred Council of Trent that the laity has taken rank and progressed in apostolic activity. . . .

Nor can one let pass unnoticed, or without recognizing its beneficent influence, that close union which, until the French Revolution, marked the mutual relations in the Catholic world of two divinely established authorities: the Church and the State. The intimacy of their relations on the common ground of public life generally created an atmosphere of Christian spirit, which rendered largely unnecessary that delicate work which clergy and laity must undertake today to safeguard the faith and assure its practical value.

At the end of the eighteenth century, a new factor came into play. On the one hand, the Constitution of the United States of America . . . , and, on the other hand, the French Revolution . . . , led to the detachment of the Church from the State. . . . This separation everywhere had for its logical conclusion the leaving of the Church to assure by her own means freedom of action, accomplishment of her mission, and defense of her rights and liberty. This was the origin of what are called the Catholic movements which . . . led the large mass of believers on to combat and to victory. Do we not see here already an initiation and introduction of the laity into the apostolate? . . .

The times were not yet ripe for a congress such as the one you have just held. How, then, did they mature in the course of this half-century? You know the answer well. Following a swifter and swifter rhythm, the cleavage which long had separated spirits and hearts into two parties, for or against God, Church, and religion, was enlarged and deepened. It established, perhaps not everywhere with equal clarity, a line of division in the very heart of peoples and families.

There is, it is true, a confused number of tepid, irresolute, and wavering souls, for whom perhaps religion still means something, but only something vague, without any influence in their lives. This amorphous mass can, as experience teaches, find itself constrained unexpectedly, one day or another, to take a decision.

So far as the Church is concerned, she has a threefold mission to fulfill for all: to raise up fervent believers to the level of present-day needs; to introduce those who hesitate on the threshold to the warm and salutary intimacy of the hearth; and to lead back those who have separated themselves from religion and whom she cannot abandon to their miserable fate.

An inspiring task for the Church! But it is one rendered more difficult by the fact that, while the Church as a whole has grown greatly, the number of clergy has not increased proportionately. Besides, the clergy must above all keep themselves free for the exercise of the sacred ministry proper to the sacerdotal state, which no one else can do for them. For that reason, assistance rendered by the laity to the apostolate is an indispensable necessity. . . .

What is the lay apostolate?

It is certainly not easy to draw an exact line of demarcation showing precisely where the true apostolate of the laity begins. Should it include, for example, the education given by the mother of a family, or by the men and women teachers engaged with holy zeal in the practice of their profession? Or the conduct of a reputable and openly Catholic doctor whose conscience never wavers when there is question of natural and divine law and who fights with all his might in defense of the Christian dignity of married persons and the sacred rights of their offspring? Should it include even the action of the Catholic statesman who sponsors a generous housing policy in favor of the less fortunate?

Many would be inclined to answer in the negative, seeing in all these examples merely the accomplishment, very laudable in itself, but obligatory, of the duties of one's state.

We recognize, however, the powerful and irreplaceable value, for the good of souls, of this ordinary performance of the duties of one's state by so many millions of conscientious and exemplary faithful.

The apostolate of the laity, in its proper sense, is without doubt to a large extent organized in Catholic Action and in other forms of apostolic activity approved by the Church; but, apart from these, there can be, and actually are, lay apostles, those men and women who see all the good to be done and the possibilities and means of doing it; and they do it with only one desire: the winning of souls to truth and grace. . . .

It is far from Our thoughts to belittle organization or to underestimate its value as a factor in the apostolate. On the contrary, We hold it in the highest esteem, especially in a world in which the adversaries of the Church descend upon Her with all the compact mass of their organization. But it must not lead to a mean exclusivism. . . .

The subordination of the lay apostolate

It is self-evident that the apostolate of the laity is subordinated to the ecclesiastical hierarchy; for the hierarchy is of divine institution. The apostolate, then, cannot be independent with regard to it. To think otherwise would be to undermine the very wall on which Christ Himself has built his Church.

Granted this, it would still be erroneous to believe that within the confines of the diocese, the traditional structure and present form of the Church place the lay apostolate in an essential parallel with the hierarchical apostolate, in such a manner that even the Bishop himself would not make the parish apostolate of the laity subject to the pastor. This the Bishop can do; and he can establish the rule that the works of the lay apostolate which are destined for the good of the parish itself should be under the pastor's authority. The Bishop has constituted the pastor the shepherd of the whole parish, and as such he is responsible for the salvation of all his sheep.

On the other hand, there may exist works of the lay apostolate which are extraparochial or even extradiocesan — We should, rather, say supraparochial and supradiocesan — according as the common good of the Church demands. That is equally true and it is not necessary to repeat it.

In Our allocution of last May 3 to Italian Catholic Action, We made it clear that the dependence of the lay apostolate with respect to the Hierarchy admits of gradations. Such dependence is strictest for Catholic Action, for Catholic Action, indeed, represents the official lay apostolate. It is an instrument in the hands of the Hierarchy. It must be, as it were, a prolongation of its arm; it is, by that very fact, essentially subject to the direction of the ecclesiastical superior. Other works of the lay apostolate, organized or not, may be left more to their free initiative, with all the latitude required by the ends to be attained. It is self-evident, however, that the initiative of the laity in the exercise of the apostolate must always remain within the bounds of orthodoxy and not oppose the lawful prescriptions of the competent ecclesiastical authorities. . . .

The scope of the lay apostolate

We cannot conclude, beloved sons and daughters, without recalling the practical work which the lay apostolate has accomplished and is accomplishing throughout the whole world in all the domains of individual and social human life. . . . We congratulate you on your resistance to that noxious tendency which exists even among Catholics and which would like to confine the Church to those questions said to be " purely religious " — not that pains are taken to know exactly what is meant by that phrase. . . . It is only too true that in certain countries the Church is constrained thus to cloister herself. Even in this case, within the four walls of the temple, she must still do, as best she can, the little that remains possible for her. She does not withdraw spontaneously or voluntarily.

Necessarily and continually, human life — both private and

social — finds itself in contact with the law and spirit of Christ. Consequently, by force of circumstance, there arises reciprocal compenetration between the religious apostolate and political action. " Political," in the highest sense of the word, means nothing else but collaboration for the good of the state. But this " good of the state " is to be understood in a very wide sense. Consequently it is on the political level that there are debated and enacted laws of the greatest import, such as those concerning marriage, the family, the child, the school, to confine Ourselves to these examples. Are these not questions which primarily interest religion? Can they leave an apostle indifferent, apathetic? . . . Catholic Action must not become a litigant in party politics. But, as We have already said to the members of the Olivaint Conference, " to the extent that it is praiseworthy to remain above contingent quarrels which poison the struggles of parties . . . to that same extent would it be blameworthy to leave the field free to persons unworthy or incapable of directing the affairs of State." . . .

Let this be Our final wish! May God deign to hear it and pour out upon you and the whole Catholic world His best graces. In testimony of this We impart to you with all Our heart, Our Apostolic Benediction.

Address of Pius XII, October 6, 1957
on

The Apostolate of the Laity [9]

. . . We speak to you at the beginning of your congress . . . with the intention of completing what We said six years ago with a few remarks on the guiding principles of the lay apostolate and on certain practical points concerning the formation and the activity of the lay apostle.

The lay apostolate derives its mandate from the hierarchy

We shall take as a starting point for these considerations one of the questions meant to define the nature of the lay apostolate, namely: " Does not the layman entrusted with teaching religion — that is, with the ' *missio canonica*,' the ecclesiastical mandate to teach — and whose teaching perhaps constitutes his only professional activity, pass by this very fact from the lay apostolate to the 'hierarchical apostolate'? "

To answer this question, it must be remembered that Christ granted His Apostles a twofold power: first, the priestly power to consecrate . . . ; second, the power to teach and govern. . . . These powers of the Apostles passed to the Pope and the bishops. The latter, through the ordination of priests, transmit to others to a precise extent the power to consecrate, while the power to teach and govern belongs to the Pope and the bishops.

When we speak of " the hierarchical apostolate " and " the lay apostolate," we must take into account a twofold distinction: first, between the Pope, bishops, and priests, on the one hand, and the mass of the laity on the other; second, among the clergy themselves, between those who possess in full the power to consecrate and govern, and other clerics. . . .

Now, in order to answer the question asked, it is important to consider the two foregoing distinctions. In the present case, it is not a matter of Holy Orders, but of the power to teach. Only those who are invested with ecclesiastical authority have the power to teach. The others, priests or laymen, collaborate with them in so far as they are trusted to teach faithfully and guide the faithful (cf. *Canons 1327–1328*).

Priests . . . and laymen also can receive the mandate for these functions, a mandate which, according to circumstances, can be the same for both. They are distinguished, however, by the fact that one is a priest and the other a layman, and that consequently the apostolate of the one is priestly and the apostolate of the other is lay. . . .

It is clear that the ordinary faithful can intend — and it is highly desirable that he should so intend — to collaborate in a more organized manner with ecclesiastical authorities and help them more effectively in their apostolic labor. He will then make himself more strictly dependent on the hierarchy, which is alone responsible before God for the government of the Church. . . .

The need for the lay apostolate

If history shows that ever since the origins of the Church laymen have taken part in the activity which the priest carries out in the service of the Church, it is true that today more than ever they must lend this collaboration with greater fervor " for building up the Body of Christ " (Eph. 4:12) in all forms of the apostolate, especially when it is a matter of making the Christian spirit penetrate all family, social, economic, and political life.

One of the reasons for this appeal to the laity lies without doubt in the lack of priests, but even in the past a priest expected the collaboration of laymen. . . . Furthermore, aside from the small number of priests, the relations between the Church and the world require the intervention of lay apostles. The consecration of the world is essentially the work of the laymen themselves, of men who are intimately a part of economic and social life and who participate in the government and in legislative assemblies. In the same way, the Catholic cells which must be created among workers in every factory and in all working environments to bring back to the Church those who have strayed from her can be constituted only by the workers themselves. . . .

The materialism and atheism of a world in which millions of believers must live in isolation requires that all should be formed into strong personalities. If not, how will they resist being led astray by the mass which surrounds them? What is true of all, is true first of all of the lay apostle who is committed not only to defend himself, but also to conquer. . . .

The place of Catholic Action in the lay apostolate

Catholic Action always bears the character of an official apostolate of laymen. Two remarks must be made here: the mandate, especially that of teaching, is not given to Catholic Action as a whole, but to its specially organized members according to the will and choice of the Hierarchy. Catholic Action must not, moreover, claim a monopoly of the lay apostolate, for along with it there remains the free lay apostolate. Individuals or groups can place themselves at the disposal of the Hierarchy and be entrusted, for a fixed or indeterminate period of time, with certain tasks for which they receive a mandate. One can therefore ask oneself if they do not also become members of Catholic Action. The important point is that the hierarchical Church, the bishops and the priests, can choose lay collaborators for themselves when they find persons capable and willing to help them.

It seems necessary here to trace, at least in its broad outline, a suggestion which has been communicated to Us very recently. It was pointed out that there prevails at the present time a regrettable and rather widespread uneasiness which finds its origin in the use of the term " Catholic Action."

This expression, in fact, is taken by some to be reserved to certain types of organized lay apostolates to which it gives, in the opinion of the public, a sort of monopoly. All organizations that do not enter into the framework of Catholic Action thus conceived, it is said, seem to have a less authentic character and a secondary importance. They seem to be supported to a lesser degree by the Hierarchy and apparently remain on the fringe of the essential apostolic effort of the laity. . . .

To solve this difficulty two practical reforms are being considered: one is a reform of terminology and the other, its corollary, is a reform of structure. First of all, it would be necessary to restore to the term " Catholic Action " its generic sense and to apply it only to all organized movements of the lay apostolate recognized as such, nationally or internationally, either by the bishops on the national plane or by the Holy See for movements aiming at having an international status. It would then be sufficient for each movement to be designated by its name and be characterized by its specific form, and not according to the common term.

The structural reform would follow the reform of terminology. All groups would belong to Catholic Action and would preserve their own name and their own autonomy, but they would form altogether, as Catholic Action, a federated unit. . . . The possible fulfillment of such a project naturally requires attentive and prolonged reflection. . . .

The formation of lay apostles

Not all Christians are called to engage in the lay apostolate in the strict sense. We have already said that the bishop should be able to choose collaborators among those whom he finds willing and able. For willingness alone is not sufficient. Lay apostles will therefore always form an elite, not because they stand apart from the others but, quite the contrary, because they are capable of attracting and influencing others. . . . [Furthermore], it is obviously necessary [for them] to accept the effort demanded by serious training. Such training, whose necessity for teachers no one doubts, is equally necessary for every lay apostle. . . .

At the present time, even the lay apostle who labors among workers in factories and business concerns needs a sound knowledge of economic, social, and political matters, and will therefore also have a knowledge of the social doctrine of the Church. It is known that there is an organization of the apostolate for men which forms its members in a "social seminary" which receives three hundred members during each winter semester and disposes of the services of twenty lecturers: university professors, judges, economists, jurists, doctors, engineers, linguists, and scientists. It seems to Us that this example is worthy of being followed.

The training of lay apostles will be taken care of by the organization of the lay apostolate itself. These may avail themselves of the help of the secular clergy and the apostolic religious orders. . . .

We wish to draw your attention particularly to one aspect of the education of young Catholics: the formation of their apostolic spirit. Instead of giving way to a slightly selfish tendency by thinking only of the salvation of their soul, they should also be made aware of their responsibilities toward others and of the ways to help them. No one doubts that prayer, sacrifice, and courageous action to win others to God constitute very definite guarantees for personal salvation. . . .

The duties of lay apostles

Regarding the application of the lay apostolate . . . , We shall limit ourselves here to referring to certain fields of the apostolate from which an urgent appeal rises at the present. . . .

The lay apostle who is involved in work in a specific district and is entrusted with a group of houses belonging to the parish must endeavor to acquire correct knowledge concerning the religious position of the inhabitants. . . . Are there marriages to be regularized among the inhabitants? Children to be baptized? What is the condition of the newsstands, bookshops, and lending libraries in the district? What material do the young folk and adults read? The complexity and often delicate character of the problems to be solved in this type of apostolate make it necessary to call upon the services of only a chosen elite having the gifts of tact and true charity.

Publishing houses and bookshops constitute a choice field for the apostolate. We are glad to hear that the majority of Catholic publishers and booksellers consider their profession as being a service to the Church. . . . Good Catholics also have an opportunity of doing good in lending libraries. The Catholic newspaperman who exercises his profession in a spirit of faith is quite naturally a lay apostle. . . .

In respect to the radio, movies, and television . . . , there is a dual task to be accomplished: avoid all elements of corruption and promote Christian values. There is by actual count an annual attendance of twelve billion in places of entertainment. Yet too many of the shows offered do not reach the cultural and moral level which one has the right to expect.

The most regrettable fact is that very often films portray a world in which men live and die as if God did not exist. In this respect, it is therefore a matter of preventing moral dangers for the faith and the Christian way of living. One could never go before God with the responsibility of having tolerated such a situation, and one must strain every effort to change it. We are therefore grateful to all those who, in the fields of radio, movies, and television, carry on a courageous, intelligent, and systematic work, which has already been rewarded with results which give grounds for serious hope. . . . In so far as television is concerned, it is indispensable for the Church to be represented on the committees entrusted with organizing programs and for Catholic experts to be among the producers. . . .

Every year twenty million young people enter the field of labor throughout the world. Among them there are Catholics, but also millions of others ready for religious formation. You must feel responsible for them all. . . . Since the climate of industrial work is dangerous to young men, the Catholic "cell" must intervene in workshops and also on trains, buses, in the families, and districts. It will act everywhere to give tone, exercise beneficial influence, and spread a new life. . . .

It would appear to Us that the lay apostolate bears three main responsibilities.

The first of these is the formation of lay apostles to make good the lack of priests in pastoral work. . . .

Secondly, exemplary Catholic men and women should be introduced into the ranks of teachers and educators from the elementary level to the university.

Thirdly, lay apostles must be introduced into economic, social, and political life. . . .

If today the consciousness of the lay apostolate is awake and if the term "lay apostle" is one of those most widely used when one speaks of the activity of the Church, it is because the collaboration of the laity with the hierarchy has never been so necessary nor practiced in such a systematic way as now. . . .

COMMENT AND EXPLICATION

"The times we live in demand action"

"We proclaim that We have no other program in the Supreme Pontificate but that 'of restoring all things in Christ.' . . .

"You see, then, Venerable Brethren, the duty that has been imposed alike upon Us and upon you of bringing back to the discipline of the Church human society now estranged from the wisdom of Christ; the Church will then subject it to Christ, and Christ to God. . . .

"It is true, Venerable Brethren, that in this arduous task of the restoration of the human race in Christ neither you nor your clergy should exclude all assistance. . . . For it is not priests alone, but all the faithful without exception who must concern themselves with the interests of God and souls — not, of course, according to their own views, but always under the direction and orders of the bishops. . . . Our predecessors have long since approved and blessed those Catholics who have banded together in societies of various kinds, but always religious in their aim. We, too, have no hesitation in awarding our praise to this great idea, and We earnestly desire to see it propagated and flourish in town and country. . . . The times we live in demand action — but action which consists entirely in observing with fidelity and zeal the divine laws and the precepts of the Church." Pius X, *E Supremi*, October 4, 1903.[10]

"Catholics ought to prefer to associate with Catholics"
"With regard to entering societies, extreme care should be taken not to be ensnared by error. And We wish to be understood as referring in a special manner to the working classes, who assuredly have the right to unite in associations for the promotion of their interests; a right acknowledged by the Church and unopposed by nature. But it is very important to take heed with whom they are to associate; lest, whilst seeking aid for the improvement of their condition, they may be imperiling far weightier interests. . . .

"Unless forced by necessity to do otherwise, Catholics ought to prefer to associate with Catholics, a course which will be very conducive to the safeguarding of their faith. As presidents of societies thus formed among themselves, it would be well to appoint either priests or upright laymen of weight and character; guided by whose counsels, they should endeavor peacefully to adopt and carry into effect such measures as may seem most advantageous to their interests, keeping in view the rules laid down by us in our Encyclical, *Rerum Novarum*." Leo XIII, *Longinqua oceani*, January 6, 1895.[11]

" As if they were obeying Him "

" This Catholic action, of whatever description it may be, will work with greater effect if all of the various associations, while preserving their individual rights, move together under one primary and directive force.

" In Italy We desire that this directive force . . . should be controlled and directed by the Bishops of the country. So let it be for other nations. . . .

" Finally, We recur again to what We have already declared and We insist upon it most solemnly, viz.: that whatever projects individuals or associations form in this matter should be done with due regard to Episcopal authority and absolutely under Episcopal guidance. Let them not be led astray by an excessive zeal in the cause of charity. If it leads them to be wanting in proper submission it is not a sincere zeal; it will not have any useful result and cannot be acceptable to God. God delights in the souls of those who put aside their own designs and obey the rulers of His Church as if they were obeying Him." Leo XIII, *Graves de communi*, January 18, 1901.[12]

There is no other teacher, no other apostolate

" Christ Our Lord entrusted the truth which he had brought from heaven to the apostles, and through them to their successors. He sent his apostles, as he had been sent by the Father (John 20:21), to teach all nations everything they had heard from him (cf. Matt. 28:19 f.). The apostles are, therefore, by divine right the true doctors and teachers in the Church. Besides the lawful successors of the apostles, namely, the Roman Pontiff for the universal Church and Bishops for the faithful entrusted to their care (cf. *Canon 1326*), there are no other teachers divinely constituted in the Church of Christ. But both the

Bishops and, first of all, the Supreme Teacher and Vicar of Christ on earth, may associate others with themselves in their work of teacher, and use their advice; they delegate to them the faculty to teach, either by special grant, or by conferring an office to which the faculty is attached (cf. *Canon 1328*). Those who are so called, teach not in their own name, nor by reason of their theological knowledge, but by reason of the mandate which they have received from the lawful Teaching Authority. Their faculty always remains subject to that Authority, nor is it ever exercised in its own right or independently." Pius XII, *Si diligis*, May 31, 1954.[13]

" As for the laity "

" As for the laity, it is clear that they can be invited by legitimate teachers and accepted as helpers in the defense of the faith. It is enough to call to mind the thousands of men and women engaged in catechetical work, and other types of the lay apostolate, all of which are highly praiseworthy and can be strenuously promoted. But all these lay apostles must be, and remain, under the authority, leadership, and watchfulness of those who by divine institution are set up as teachers of Christ's Church." Pius XII, *Si diligis*, May 31, 1954.[14]

Free to think for oneself, provided . . .

" It is quite natural for people to think differently in doubtful questions. . . . To whatever opinion a man's judgment may incline, if the matter is yet open to discussion, let him keep it, provided his mental attitude is such that he is ready to yield if the Holy See should otherwise decide." Leo XIII, *Graves de communi*, January 18, 1901.[15]

There is no " lay theology "

" Recently what is called ' lay theology ' has sprung up and spread to various places, and a new class of ' lay theologian ' has emerged, which claims to be *sui juris*. . . . These professors distinguish their teaching authority from, and in a certain way set it up against, the public Teaching Authority of the Church; at times, in order to justify their position, they appeal to the charismatic gifts of teaching and of interpreting prophecy, which are mentioned more than once in the New Testament, especially in the Pauline Epistles (e.g., Rom. 12:6 f.; I Cor. 12:28-30); they appeal to history, which from the beginning of the Christian religion down to today presents so many names of laymen who for the good of souls have taught the truth of Christ orally and in writing, though not called to this by the Bishops and without having asked or received the sacred teaching authority, led on by their own inward impulse and apostolic zeal. Nevertheless it is necessary to maintain to the contrary that there never has been, there is not now, and there never will be in the Church a legitimate teaching authority of the laity withdrawn by God from the authority, guidance, and watchfulness of the sacred Teaching Authority; in fact, the very denial of submission offers a convincing proof and criterion that laymen who thus speak and act are not guided by the Spirit of God and of Christ." Pius XII, *Si diligis*, May 31, 1954.[16]

Even " if their doctrines were free from error "

" If their doctrines were free from error, it would, nevertheless, be a grave failure in Catholic discipline to withdraw themselves obstinately from the direction of those who have received from heaven the mission to guide individuals and societies in the straight way of truth and well-doing." Pius X, *Condemnation of the* Sillon, August 25, 1910.[17]

It is not permissible " to deviate even a hairsbreadth "
"It is not lawful . . . to stray from the inflexible lines of Christian principles, which are the bases of political and social life and which the Church has repeatedly and with great clarity expounded to men of our times. . . . By disposition of Divine Providence the Catholic Church has formulated and promulgated its social doctrine. She points the path to be followed, and no fear of losing possessions or of temporal gains, of appearing less in harmony with modern civilization or less national and social, could authorize true Christians to deviate even a hairsbreadth from this path." Pius XII, address to the College of Cardinals, June 2, 1947.[18]

" A vast and fertile field for action "
"Is it not as ridiculous as it is hateful to accuse the clergy of keeping the laity in humiliating inactivity? Let the laity turn its attention to the family, social and scholastic questions; let it become active in science or art, literature or the radio and cinema; let it engage in political campaigns for the election of the legislative bodies or for the definition of their powers and their constitutional attributes. Everywhere Catholic laymen will find open to them a vast and fertile field for action." Pius XII, address to the members of the Christian Workers' Movement of Belgium, September 11, 1949.[19]

" Your place is in the vanguard "
"In the battle of the day your place is in the vanguard, fighting at the front. The timid and those who are afraid to come out into the open are very close to becoming

deserters and traitors. He is a deserter and a traitor who gives his material support, his services, his talents, aid or votes to parties and to forces which deny God, which put might in the place of right, and threats and terror in the place of liberty, which make of lying, opposition, and incitement of the masses, so many weapons of their policy, thus rendering national and international peace impossible." Pius XII, Christmas message, December 24, 1947.[20]

" Make yourselves felt "

" You are not weak! Remain, therefore, conscious of your strength and also of your sacred responsibility to make your Christian convictions felt in public life. . . . Make yourselves felt, use your rights and your inner riches, in legislation and administration, in marriage and in the family, in education and in the schools, in the saving of the workers from the danger of falling into atheistic materialism." Pius XII, address to the Congress of Swiss Catholics, September 4, 1949.[21]

The apostolate of the pen

" Much may be contributed by those who have devoted themselves to writing, and in particular by those who are engaged in the daily press. . . . Since the thirst for reading and knowledge is so vehement and widespread amongst you, and since, according to circumstances, it can be productive either of good or evil, every effort should be made to increase the number of intelligent and well-disposed writers who take religion for their guide and virtue for their constant companion. And this seems all the more necessary in America, on account of the familiar intercourse and intimacy between Catholics and those who are estranged from the Catholic name, a condition of things which certainly exacts from our people great cir-

cumspection and more than ordinary firmness. It is necessary to instruct, admonish, strengthen, and urge them on
to the pursuit of virtue and to the faithful observance,
amid so many occasions of stumbling, of their duties toward the Church. It is, of course, the proper function of the
clergy to devote their care and energies to this great work:
but the age and the country require that journalists
should be equally zealous in this same cause, and labor
in it to the full extent of their powers. Let them, however,
seriously reflect that their writings, if not positively preju-
dicial to religion, will surely be of slight service to it unless
in concord of mind they all seek the same end. They who
desire to be of real service to the Church, and with their
pens heartily to defend the Catholic cause, should carry
on the conflict with perfect unanimity and, as it were,
with serried ranks, for they rather inflict than repel war,
if they waste their strength by discord. . . . Let them,
then, be mindful of their duty, and not overstep the proper
limits of moderation. The bishops, placed in the lofty position of authority, are to be obeyed, and suitable honor
befitting the magnitude and sanctity of their office should
be paid to them." Leo XIII, *Longinqua oceani*, January 6,
1895.[22]

VI

CONCLUDING OBSERVATIONS

IT SHOULD be clear from the foregoing documents that for Roman Catholics obedience to the constituted authority of the church is the great virtue and disobedience the great sin, for the Bishop of Rome holds upon earth the place of Almighty God and to be obedient to him is to be obedient to God. Nor is this obedience restricted to "matters strictly religious." Pius XII said that there are sometimes statesmen in high office who say: "We are perfectly willing to see, to listen to, and to approach Bishops and priests in their churches, and regarding matters within their authority; but in places of official and public business, where matters of this life are dealt with and decided, we have no wish to see them or to listen to what they say. For there, it is we laymen, and not the clergy — no matter of what rank or qualification — who are the legitimate judges." But, says Pius XII, "We must take an open and firm stand against errors of this kind." [1]

There are interesting corollaries to this insistence upon the necessity of obedience. While for good and compelling reasons discipline at times may be relaxed and disobedience tolerated; when the chips are down on an important issue, the reins are tightened and the full powers of the church are brought into play to enforce obedience. Furthermore, in the application of its teaching, the Roman

Church must always balance the respective "goods" and "evils" involved in a particular situation. According to the most authoritative Roman moral theology, the sin of an act is not in the sin itself, but in the conscious rebellion of the actor against the laws of the church in committing the act. If a person is in ignorance, he does not sin. " A confessor who discovers such ignorance in his laity must consider carefully. If he informs the penitent that to do thus and so is against the church's teaching when he is morally certain that the man will continue to act so anyway, he is himself guilty of leading the man into sin. Therefore, in normal circumstances, the priest should not inform his ignorant penitents of the wrongness of those actions that are likely to continue to prove too tempting to them." To so inform them would only serve to convert their ignorant misdemeanors into conscious sin. But when some great evil would be incurred or some greater good sacrificed or endangered — when the interests of the church, for example, are involved — by such ignorance, then it becomes the obligation of the confessor to inform the conscience and to instruct the penitent as to his duty, even though he runs the risk of leading him into moral sin.[2] It is only within this context that one can understand the failure of the Roman Church to make clear to the faithful the full implications of its teaching on many issues of public concern. To do so might drive some of the faithful to open rebellion, whereas their support can be gained if the full implications are not spelled out. It is enough to face the issues one by one as occasion warrants and as conditions give some promise of success, without exposing the full obedience that is ultimately to be required; for this procedure offers the possibility of greater " good " being done.

The insistence upon obedience — the Roman obedience — springs from an essentially utopian vision. The Roman Catholic believes that God wills that complete harmony shall prevail in all the facets of human existence. Unlike the Protestant who believes that there must be conflict and contradiction in this present world due to man's fallen estate and who believes that the resolution of all ambiguities and the harmonization of all powers and concerns must await the reconciliation of all things in God's final act of redemption, the Roman Catholic believes that Christ now rules this present world in the fullness of his power, that all the ambiguities of human existence have been fully resolved, and that the remaining contradictions and conflicts can be eliminated by the proper ordering of life in accordance with his clear teaching. The notion that our understanding of God's revelation may be partial and even perverted by self-concern, the notion that the oneness of the church may be only imperfectly made manifest, the notion that the church in any of its institutional forms wears the countenance of a sinner and stands under judgment, the notion that only proximate justice and harmony can be secured by various devices of checks and balances — all these are foreign to Roman Catholic thinking.

This utopian concept of the full harmony that God wills shall prevail in this present world leads to several very practical and pragmatic conclusions. If the church in an institutional sense is to be characterized by perfect harmony and oneness, then no mere majority decision in interpreting the mind and will of Christ will do. It is essential that one person shall be " the head of all " to adjudicate the differences that may arise, and it is equally essential — if the unity is to be in Christ — that he shall have full power from Christ to teach and to rule in his stead.

In the same manner, if full harmony is to prevail in the temporal order, it is essential that there shall be a "ruling authority over all" and that it shall be "entrusted with the power to command with real and effective authority." [3] It likewise follows, if perfect harmony is to prevail between these two ruling authorities, that one of them must take precedence in areas of possible conflict and have the power to determine what falls within the area of its competence to command.[4] The conflicts of the economic order are subjected to the same type of resolution. The interests of the employer and of the employee are assumed to be identical, and employers and employees are to gather in industry councils to identify their true interest and to arrive at a mutually advantageous agreement. If through ineptness they should fail to achieve harmonious agreement, the state is then to intervene to resolve the conflict.[5] In the family, to the same end that harmony shall prevail, it is held that God has ordained that the wife shall be subject to the husband.[6] Thus throughout society there is a descending hierarchy of authority designed to secure and preserve the "natural" unity and concord of mankind.

Under the impact of the necessity for lay witness and action, the Roman Catholic conception of the church has tended to undergo a shift of emphasis. Whereas the tendency had been to define the church in terms of the hierarchy, much greater attention is now being given to the concept of the church as a people. Thus Pius XII, speaking of the indispensable role of the laity in shaping the life of society, has said:

"Considered from this angle, the Church may be called the assembly of those who, under the supernatural influence of grace, in the perfection of their personal dignity as sons of God and in the harmonious development of all

human inclinations and energies, build the powerful structure of human intercourse.

"Under this aspect, Venerable Brethren, the faithful,
and more precisely the laity, are in the front line of the
Church's life; for them the Church is the vital principle of
human society. Accordingly, they — especially they —
must have an ever-clearer sense not only of belonging to
the Church, but of being the Church, the community of
the faithful on earth under the guidance of the common
head, the Pope, and of the Bishops in communion with
him." [7]

An incipient tendency can be detected here to move
somewhat haltingly in the direction of the Reformation
concept of the church. Furthermore, if the necessities of
Catholic Action have led to a heightened awareness of the
laity as a constituent element of the church, the fostering
of the lay apostolate also has overtones reminiscent of the
Protestant doctrines of the priesthood of believers and the
universality of the Christian vocation. Nevertheless, from
the Protestant perspective both tendencies are abortive,
being inhibited, frustrated, and shackled at a crucial point.

For the faithful to be fully the church and for the believers to be fully priests, they must have the full apostolate. Nor does it seem possible for there to be a fully responsible discipleship in the life of the world on any other
basis. This, as we have seen, is the crucial point that Roman
Catholicism is unable to concede. Roman Catholicism
insists that the apostolate belongs to the hierarchy, not
even to the clergy as a whole, and that any apostolate of
the laity must be in subordination and in full obedience to
the hierarchy.

This is the fundamental issue at stake between Protestantism and Roman Catholicism. Protestants believe that

the apostolate does reside in the whole company of the faithful and that every Christian is called and commissioned and sent to bear testimony to Christ. The Great Commission, to be sure, was spoken to the disciples, but at the time when it was spoken the disciples constituted the whole body of the faithful. It seems obvious to Protestants that the Great Commission was addressed to all faithful Christians. The whole consequence of being one with Christ, Luther observed, is that we are also one among ourselves. This would seem to be the clear teaching of the New Testament.

The implications of this point of view with regard to any claims that would posit a unique authority for the clergy is immediately apparent. If the apostolate belongs to the church, and if the church is the faithful, and if all the faithful are called to be priests, the only distinction between the clergy and the laity is a distinction of function. The clergy act for the laity in a *representative* capacity. In other respects, the clergyman is just another believer of the same rank as the generality of " priests " or " ministers " who constitute the body of the church. In a very real sense, in the Protestant understanding of the Christian faith, there is no laity; all are priests. It is for this reason that Protestants regarded the suppressed " Worker-Priest " movement in France as something less than an innovation. For whenever a Protestant minister relinquishes his pastoral responsibilities to take a job in a factory, he simply reverts to the role of the other worker-priests — his fellow believers — who have been there on the assembly line or at the workbench all the time.

A further implication of this fundamental issue is to be found in the Protestant doctrine of the universality of the Christian vocation. It has been suggested that on the basis

of the obedience that must be yielded to papal direction a
fully responsible discipleship is impossible. It is only a
passive activism that the Roman Church seeks of the laity
in their family, civic, and vocational life. They do not
have the responsibility of weighing alternatives and of
making real decisions, of determining before God where
their specific duty lies. The important decisions are made
for them, the way is charted in detail, and their only responsibility is to walk therein. It is frequently asserted
that the conscience of a Roman Catholic is not coerced,
that a Roman Catholic is as free as his non-Roman neighbors. In a sense this is true, but only in a very limited
sense. His conscience is his own at only one point, in terms
of his freedom to accept or to reject the Roman obedience.
Once he has made this decision and has accepted the
authority of the church, his conscience henceforth is in
the custody of his confessor. This means, for example, that
he is able to participate only to a limited extent in the
discussion and debate of the democratic process. On
merely " technical " questions he is free to make up his
own mind, but on most questions that involve significant
issues he is apt to find that the matter has already been
decided by the church and that he, therefore, has nothing to learn from the discussion. There are no new in-
sights to be gained, no new perspectives to be revealed,
no new considerations to be disclosed, no new alternatives
to be brought forth. The issue is settled not by the dictates of his own conscience in the light of his own Christian convictions but by the authority of the church. It
must be remembered, of course, that it may not always be
expedient for the confessor to inform the conscience of
the penitent as to his duty, and thus in certain situations —
in the United States, for example — a rather extensive

freedom of decision may be permitted.

There has been a very earnest and a very sincere effort by some of the more liberal-minded Roman Catholic theologians to demonstrate that Roman Catholic doctrine can be reconciled with the practices and customs of a democratic society, and of course it can be so reconciled. But some things have been said in this endeavor that would seem to be difficult to defend. It has been said, for example, that the papal condemnation of basic democratic principles was directed against the type of " godless " democracy to be found in France, the implication being that no general condemnation of democratic doctrine was intended. Laying aside the question as to whether or not French democracy may be truly described as " godless " (an accusation deriving its main force from the French government's act in disestablishing the church), there were other democracies in existence — in the United States, in Great Britain, in Switzerland, and elsewhere. Pius XI has stated that it is unworthy of the faithful to seek to evade the force of papal teaching by assuming that " the Church, sent by God to teach and guide all nations, is not conversant with present affairs and circumstances." [8] It would seem quite certain that if no general condemnation were intended, the usual careful qualifications — so characteristic of papal documents — would have been introduced.

A second point that is frequently made is that the Roman Church exists in many different lands and must adapt itself to many different situations and forms of government. Furthermore, it is pointed out, not all peoples are capable of self-government. Thus it would be wrong to expect Roman Catholicism to take a rigid and doctrinaire stand in favor of democracy. It is true, of course, that not all peoples are capable of immediate self-government; the "trusteeship" territories administered under the direction of the United Nations is one recognition of this fact. It is also true that the Roman Catholic Church must adapt itself to different situations in different lands. But the crucial question is from what "norm" are the adaptations to be made. The "norm" of Roman Catholic political theory, "the form and character of the state were it governed according to the principles of Christian philosophy," the ultimate goal to be sought in the right ordering of political life, as we have seen, is far removed from what is commonly understood by democracy. While recognizing the need to make adjustments and adaptations to the necessities of specific situations, the ordinary citizen in a democracy would feel much more secure if such adjustments and adaptations were made from a "norm" that incorporated the essential features of the Bill of Rights rather than the reverse. The anxieties and suspicions of many sincere persons would be mitigated if the ultimate goal to be sought included the basic guarantees of freedom of speech, freedom of assembly, freedom of the press, and freedom of religion.

Most of the attempts by Roman Catholics to find a basis for democratic freedom in the teaching of the church operate within the framework of secondary considerations. Father Robert C. Harnett, for example, posed the question that he said Protestants often raise: "We are not concerned so much with what you would do, as a matter of policy, if you became a majority, as with what your doctrine would *require* you to do." To this he responded by saying: "What would our doctrine require us to do? The best answer to this question in English, so far as I know, is Dr. J. Pohle's article on 'Toleration' in *The*

Catholic Encyclopedia." He then cites four quotations from the article and concludes: " This much is clear: there is no agreed-upon Catholic doctrine which requires that Catholics, should they ever become a majority in the United States, must curtail the religious freedom of their non-Catholic fellow Americans." The key words, of course, are *require* (which Father Harnett italicized) and *must.* Actually all that the article in *The Catholic Encyclopedia* says is that under certain conditions a degree of toleration or even complete religious freedom is permissible and may be necessary. But " dogmatic " toleration — a belief in toleration as a fundamental principle of government — is ruled out. Toleration can be defended only on the basis of prudential considerations arising out of the contingencies of particular circumstances.[9] This, of course, is no more than a restatement of the point made by Leo XIII in " The Christian Constitution of States " that when there is need to make an adjustment " for the sake of securing some great good or of hindering some great evil," the church will give " signal proof of her motherly love by showing the greatest possible kindliness and indulgence."

Some Roman Catholic theologians, however, have sought to find a more positive basis for democratic liberties. Father John Courtney Murray, of Woodstock College, is perhaps the most distinguished of the theologians engaged in this endeavor. He gives a reverse twist to the argument, and, while he succeeds in providing a positive support for both civil and religious liberties, he confesses that they are not to be regarded as " unalienable " rights. They are always subject to modification in terms of the requirements imposed by the secondary considerations spelled out in the concept of the common good.

The religious freedom of individuals, Father Murray maintains, is not a special category of freedom — " privileged and absolute." It is simply an aspect of civil liberties in general that find their sanction in the natural law. ". . . the right of religious propaganda and the right of religious organization are simply aspects of the general human rights of free association and of free discussion. They have no natural foundation separate from the foundation of these more general rights, nor have they any privileged absolutism. The natural law grants no more privileged right to organize for religious purposes than to organize for economic purposes. And, simply because an idea is religious, it has from the natural law no more absolute right to be propagated than if it were merely political." [10]

The right of religious propaganda and the right of religious association are not privileged and absolute because all natural rights are limited by the requirements of the common good. Thus they are always subject to restriction and denial within the scope of what the Roman Catholic Church — the only competent and authoritative interpreter of the natural law — considers to be the common good. While conscience cannot be coerced, religious activity and expression may be restricted, for the common good includes man's moral and spiritual welfare. Liberty thus limited is true liberty — liberty of teaching and publishing and organizing to propagate that which is true and thus conducive to the attainment of man's ultimate supernatural end.

Of quite a different category from the provisional rights of individuals and other religious bodies are the rights of the Roman Catholic Church. It has a set of liberties that other faiths do not possess, liberties based upon positive divine law which supersedes and transcends the limited natural rights common to all. The Roman Catholic Church, says Murray, has special liberties that " are not an aspect of political liberty, but *sui generis*," because the Roman Catholic Church is " a society that is itself juridically perfect, independent in its own sphere . . . , and dowered with rights from another source (positive divine law) than that which is the first source of political liberties (the law of nature)." By definition, the unique rights of the Roman Catholic Church cannot conflict with the common good, and they are absolute and unalienable because they are conferred directly upon the Roman Church by God. There is in Father Murray's reinterpretation of Roman political theory a shift in the role assigned to secondary considerations, but in terms of the practical conclusions that may be drawn therefrom it would seem to be indistinguishable from the conclusions spelled out by Leo XIII. Even if this line of thought with its subsidiary but highly qualified support for civil and religious liberty were to become the official teaching of the church, it would offer scant comfort to non-Romanists seeking solid guarantees for their own freedom.[11]

Roman Catholic apologists, such as the editor of *The Commonweal*, from time to time have sought to reassure American Protestants and other non-Romanists by citing some such statement as that of the late Archbishop McNicholas of Cincinnati that should Roman Catholics become a majority in the United States they would " not seek a union of Church and State " but " then, as now, uphold the Constitution and all its Amendments." [12] Unfortunately, from the point of view of Roman Catholic dogma, the assurance even of an archbishop is not sufficient to allay the disquiet of their fellow citizens. The

"Worker-Priest" movement in France had episcopal authorization and support, but the practically unanimous support of the French hierarchy did not suffice to prevent the movement from being condemned and suppressed. The voice that counts is the voice of Rome. The minimum assurance that would serve to relieve the often unexpressed anxieties of many concerning the ultimate intentions of the Roman Catholic Church would seem, therefore, to be a papal declaration that it is at least *permissible* for a Roman Catholic to accept and defend, on the basis of principle as "unalienable" rights of all Americans, the fundamental guarantees embodied in the Bill of Rights.

It does not seem likely that such a pronouncement will be forthcoming, for the tendency has been in the direction of a more rigid insistence upon strict adherence to papal teaching rather than of a greater latitude of interpretation. The reins have been progressively tightened and "liberalizing" tendencies have been repeatedly condemned, the most recent instance being the spirited reaffirmation in the papal allocution of May 31, 1954, of the condemnations pronounced in *Humani Generis*.[13] The Roman Catholic "liberals" continue to live in hope, but it is a hope that has been repeatedly shattered and that requires of them ever more subtle rationalizations. Therein lie both the pathos and the tragedy of their position.

A final observation is in order. There are many aspects of Roman Catholicism — the sacraments and sacramentals, pious practices and patterns of devotion, for example — that have not been included in this volume. This is the result of a quite deliberate narrowing of focus. The intention has been to identify that which is distinctive of Roman Catholicism, that which makes one a Roman Catholic, and to illustrate its implications. Not even the great issue posed by the doctrine of "justification by faith alone" is directly relevant to this concern, for it is "the Roman obedience" rather than any conception of salvation by accumulated merits that distinguishes the Roman Catholic from all others who claim the name of Christian. The implications of the Roman obedience could have been further illustrated in many other areas of common concern — most notably in the family, in the economic order, and in the field of education. But this would have been to make a large book of what was quite explicitly designed to be a small one. Conversation is important, and the first essential for fruitful conversation is to understand one another so that the real issues may be identified. If this book helps Protestants to better understand Roman Catholicism, it will have served its purpose, and it may thereby make some small contribution to mutual understanding.

APPENDIXES

APPENDIX A

THE CONSOLIDATION OF PAPAL CONTROL
UNDER PIUS X

THREE men have been largely responsible for the shaping of modern Roman Catholicism. The course was set by Pius IX (1846–1878) when he provided the Roman Catholic Church with its definitive dogmatic basis in the Constitution that he promulgated at the Vatican Council in 1870. Leo XIII (1878–1903), taking his stance upon the foundation provided by Pius IX, spelled out for the faithful the basic philosophy of the church in relationship to the political, social, and intellectual orders; giving major attention, to be sure, to the political order and devising the strategy by which the church could operate to secure its ends within the context of a democratic society. It was left to Pius X (1903–1914) to introduce into the church further measures of practical control that would render it a more efficient and well-disciplined instrument for the achievement of the goal that had been set before the church by his two predecessors.

Adopting as his slogan " the restoration of all things in Christ," Pius X set forth his program in his first encyclical letter, *E Supremi,* October 4, 1903.[1] His immediate objective was to reduce both the clergy and the laity to full obedience so that the ultimate objective of bringing human society back to the discipline of the church might be attained. He moved with dispatch on both these fronts, but, as a practical ecclesiastical administrator, he also recognized that the whole administrative machinery of the church needed to be put on a more efficient basis. This was especially true of the organization of the papal court — the Roman Curia. A partial reorganization was effected on December 7, 1903; further reforms were introduced in 1904 and 1906; and finally the Curia was given a new constitution, which codified and completed the piecemeal reorganization, on June 29, 1908.[2] Out of a similar concern, Pius X directed that the canon law be recodified.

In his encyclical letter *E Supremi,* Pius X had acknowledged that the summons to the laity to participate in the apostolate of the church had been " a great idea," for the times demanded action — action that only the laity could take. But, as was true of his predecessors, he was insistent that it must be " action which consists entirely in observing with fidelity and zeal the divine laws and precepts of the Church." To make certain that Catholic Action should be fully subordinated to " the direction and orders of the bishops," he issued on December 18, 1903 a *motu proprio* containing nineteen rules to govern the activities of Catholic Action.[3] Two years later these rules were further elaborated and detailed in the encyclical *Il fermo proposito* (June 11, 1905).

Neither administrative reorganization nor the tightening of control over the laity was the most urgent concern of Pius X. In spite of the Vatican decrees many of the clergy remained restive. There were " modernists " among them who questioned both the definition that had been given the church and the extent of its teaching authority. In *E Supremi,* Pius X stated that the " first care " of the

bishops must be the proper "formation" of the priesthood
to prevent "the members of the clergy from being drawn
to the snares of a certain new and fallacious science,
which savoreth not of Christ, but with masked and cunning arguments strives to open the door to the errors of
rationalism and semirationalism." This emphasis upon the
proper formation of the priesthood was to be the recurrent
theme of the greater portion of his subsequent encyclicals,
whether they celebrated the virtues of the saints or took
cognizance of the fiftieth anniversary of his own ordination to the priesthood.[4]

The first steps that Pius X took in the offensive to
counter the threat posed by the self-assertiveness of the
clergy and particularly of theological professors were the
reorganization of the Biblical Commission and a series of
decrees issued by the Index on December 16, 1903, condemning five books by Alfred Loisy, one of the most distinguished proponents of the so-called "modernist"
views.[5] Further action was delayed because of preoccupa-
tion with the political controversy in which the church had
become embroiled in France, but in 1906 disciplinary
action was renewed and in 1907 "modernism" was formally defined and condemned in a new syllabus of errors,
Lamentabili, and in the encyclical letter *Pascendi*.[6]

Lamentabili was a decree of the Inquisition condemning
sixty-five specific propositions, and *Pascendi* contained a
full exposition of the views of modernism, presenting it
as a conspiracy to propagate heresy in the church, and
spelling out the measures to be adopted in every diocese
to stamp it out. Leo XIII's directive which made Thomism
the official philosophy of the church was reaffirmed, and a
thorough instruction in the Thomist system was enjoined.
Directions were given for the selection of professors, the

supervision of publications, the utilization of censorship, and the holding of conferences. But the major instrument of episcopal control was to be a system of espionage, with " councils of vigilance," or " watch committees," in every diocese to detect and extirpate errors. To insure that the instructions would be carried out, each bishop was ordered to make a triennial report to the papacy of actions taken and results obtained. Later in the same year, on November 18, 1907, a decree of the Biblical Commission exhorted the bishops to renewed vigilance over all teachers, especially those in seminaries, and directed that if any be found lacking in docility to the prescriptions of the Apostolic See, they should be removed forthwith from their teaching office. To give added weight to the papal directives, this decision decreed that the condemnations pronounced in both *Lamentabili* and *Pascendi* represented the infallible teaching of the Holy See. " In order to check the daily increasing audacity of many modernists who are endeavoring by all kinds of sophistry and devices to detract from the force and efficacy not only of the decree *Lamentabili sane exitu* issued by our order by the Holy Roman and Universal Inquisition on July 3, of the present year, but also of our encyclical letter *Pascendi Dominici gregis* given on September 8 of this same year, We do by our apostolic authority repeat and confirm both that decree of the Supreme Sacred Congregation and those encyclical letters of Ours, adding the penalty of excommunication against their contradictors, and this We declare and decree that should anybody, which may God forbid, be so rash as to defend any one of the propositions, opinions, or teachings condemned in these documents he falls, *ipso facto*, under the censure contained under the chapter ' *Docentes* ' of the constitution *Apostolicae Sedis*, which is the first among the excommunications *latae sententiae,* simply reserved to the Roman Pontiff." [7]

The culminating action of Pius X in his effort to devise practical means to make certain that the clergy would be fully obedient to papal control came in 1910 when he issued a *motu proprio* " establishing certain laws for the driving out of the danger of modernism." [8] In this decree, he speaks again of the " cunning " of the modernists and of their " secret " conspiracy to subvert the church, recalls the teaching of *Pascendi,* quotes at length the instructions to the bishops contained therein, and renews the call for episcopal vigilance, zeal, and firmness in stamping out this " pest." To this end, he provides further instructions. He deals first with students in seminaries and religious institutes, directing that they shall be closely observed to note, among other things, whether or not they exhibit a proper spirit of docility. If not, and if they do not reform after one or two admonitions, they are to be expelled. Students are also to be reminded of the qualities essential for ecclesiastical promotion. Furthermore, they are not to be permitted to read any periodicals or journals, for this would serve to distract them from their studies and it has also been a means whereby the infection of modernism has spread. The professors in the seminaries, for their part, must submit to the bishop each year the text they propose to use, and their actual teaching is to be checked each year to determine whether or not it conforms to sound doctrine. If it does not, they are to be immediately removed from their post. The major device that the bishops were directed to use, however, is the so-called " antimodernist " oath that all the clergy henceforth were to be required to take and to reaffirm whenever they were instituted to a new office. The requirement for seminary professors was even more rigid, for they are required to make an annual public profession of the oath. The oath, somewhat abridged, is as follows:

" I, . . . , firmly hold and accept each and every definition of the unerring teaching of the Church, with all she has maintained and declared, but especially those points of doctrine which expressly combat the errors of our time. In the first place, I profess my belief that God, the beginning and the end of all, can be surely known and also proved to exist by the natural light of reason from the things that are made, that is, from the visible works of the creation as a cause from its effects. Next I recognize and acknowledge the external arguments of revelations, that is, divine facts, especially miracles and prophecies, as the surest signs of the divine origin of the Christian religion, and I hold that these are specially suited to the understanding of every age and of all men, even of our times. Thirdly, I likewise hold with firm faith that the Church, the guardian and exponent of the revealed Word, was proximately and directly founded by Christ Himself, the true person of history, while He dwelt amongst us, and that she was also built upon Peter, the Prince of the Apostolic Hierarchy, and upon his successors to the end of time. Fourthly, I sincerely receive the teaching of faith as transmitted in the same sense and meaning right down to us; and, therefore, I wholly reject the heretical notion of the evolution of dogmas, which pass from one sense to another alien to that the Church held from the start; and I likewise condemn every error whereby is substituted for the divine deposit, entrusted by Christ to

His spouse and by her to be faithfully guarded, a
philosophic system or a creation of the human conscience, gradually refined by the striving of men and
finally to be perfected hereafter by indefinite progress. . . .

" I further, with all due reverence, submit and with
my whole mind adhere to all the condemnations,
declarations and directions contained in the encyclical
letter *Pascendi* and in the decree *Lamentabili,* particularly regarding what is called the history of
dogma.

" I also reject the error of those who allege that
the faith proposed by the Church may be in conflict
with history and that Catholic dogmas in the sense
in which they are now understood cannot be harmo-
nized with the more truthful ' origins ' of Christianity. . . .

" Finally and in general, I declare myself to be far
removed from the error of the modernists. . . .
Wherefore most firmly I retain and to my last breath
will I retain the faith of the Fathers of the Church
concerning the sure endowment of truth, which is,
has been and ever will be in the succession of the
episcopate from the Apostles (St. Irenaeus IV, c.
26); not in such a way that we may hold what seems
best and most fitting according to the refinement of
each age, but that we never in any different wise
understand the absolute and unchangeable truth
preached from the beginning by the Apostles. (*Prae-
script,* c. 28.)

" All this I promise that I will faithfully, entirely
and sincerely keep and inviolably guard, and from
this never in teaching or howsoever by word or writ-

ing in the least depart. So I promise, so I swear, so help me God, etc." [9]

The various administrative devices that Pius X directed the bishops to adopt were eminently successful in achieving the end that he pursued with such unremitting zeal. As a result of his efforts, papal control over the church was made secure at every point. The theologians, to be sure, from time to time, as in the encyclical letter *Humani Generis* of 1950, have had to be reminded of the limits imposed by papal teaching; and it has been felt necessary on occasion, as in the papal allocution *Si diligis* of 1954, to direct the bishops to make sure that the vigilance of the diocesan "watch committees" was not relaxed. The fact that the rebukes of *Humani Generis* were accepted without protest or dissent is eloquent testimony to the effectiveness of Pius X's measures in inculcating a spirit of docility. What may be an equally clear indication of the present temper of the Roman Catholic Church is the fact that of all the modern Roman Pontiff's it was the one most distinguished for his practical administrative talents, Pius X, who was canonized as a saint on May 31, 1954. And it was quite in keeping with the spirit of Pius X that Pius XII should have utilized this occasion to address the assembled cardinals, archbishops, and bishops on the duty of obedience to the Holy See.

APPENDIX B

ESSENTIAL CHARACTERISTICS OF EX CATHEDRA PRONOUNCEMENTS

There is no authoritative definition as to what constitutes an infallible ex cathedra papal pronouncement, and it is probable that the Roman Catholic Church is purposely ambiguous at this point. It is generally assumed, however, that ex cathedra pronouncements differ from other pronouncements in three essential respects.[1] First of all, the matter must be one of faith or morals. Secondly, some such word as " declare," " define," or " pronounce " would seem to be necessary. Thirdly, sanctions in the form of the obligation to believe and the censures incurred through disbelief must be definitely stated. No one questions the fact that the following pronouncements are among those which may definitely be regarded by Roman Catholics as containing infallible definitions of the faith: the promulgation of the dogma of the Immaculate Conception in 1854; the Constitution of the Faith and the Constitution of the Church, both of which were issued at the Vatican Council in 1870; the decree *Lamentabili* and the encyclical *Pascendi* of 1907; and the promulgation of the dogma of the Assumption of Mary in 1950. There has been a disposition on the part of some to regard the *Syllabus of Errors* of 1864 as falling within the scope of infallible teaching, but others entertain doubt at this point, while acknowledging that, whether infallible or not, the *Syllabus* is bind-

173

ing on all Roman Catholics and requires their internal assent. There has been similar controversy over the doctrinal force of the encyclicals in general — a controversy that is now being extended to include the papal allocutions that have become increasingly popular as a means through which papal teaching is expressed. Most Roman Catholics, it would seem, are right in regarding this whole controversy as purely academic, since obedience must be yielded just as readily to the ordinary pronouncements as to the extraordinary infallible teaching.

SUGGESTIONS FOR FURTHER READING

For those who wish to pursue further reading on this subject, the available literature is almost limitless. Some persons may wish preliminary guidance in the form of specific suggestions.

Two little books that will quickly serve to provide perspective are Winthrop S. Hudson, *The Story of the Christian Church* (Harper & Brothers, 1958), and J. H. Nichols, *A Short Primer for Protestants* (A Reflection Book, Association Press, 1957). A detailed account of the redefinition of Roman Catholicism at the Vatican Council of 1870 and an analysis of its significance is provided by Geddes MacGregor, *The Vatican Revolution* (The Beacon Press, Inc., 1957). A most useful aid in locating where papal encyclicals have been published is M. C. Carlen, *A Guide to the Encyclicals of the Roman Pontiffs from Leo XIII to the Present Day, 1878–1937* (The H. W. Wilson Company, 1939). This is supplemented by another volume by the same author, *Guide to the Documents of Pius XII, 1939–1949* (The Newman Press, 1951).

There are several useful interpretations of Roman Catholicism from a Protestant point of view: Karl Heim, *Spirit and Truth* (Lutterworth Press, London, 1935); Richard Hanson and Reginald Fuller, *The Church of Rome: A Dissuasive* (S. C. M. Press, Ltd., London, 1948); C. Anderson Scott, *Romanism and the Gospel* (The Westminster Press, 1946). The points of agreement and disagreement between Protestantism and Roman Catholicism are discussed with insight by K. E. Skydsgaard, *One in Christ* (Muhlenberg Press, 1957).

An incisive and illuminating study of the relationship of both Roman Catholicism and Protestantism to the political developments of the last century and a half has been made by J. H. Nichols, *Democracy and the Churches* (The Westminster Press, 1951). Professor Nichols speaks bluntly of the record of Roman Catholicism, but he speaks no less bluntly of Protestantism. A statement of the case for the separation of church and state from a Protestant point of view will be found in Winthrop S. Hudson, *The Great Tradition of the American Churches* (Harper & Brothers, 1953).

Detailed information concerning the more conspicuous aspects of Roman Catholicism is to be found in Stanley I. Stuber, *Primer on Roman Catholicism for Protestants* (Association Press, 1953). A mine of information concerning the historical origins of many facets of Roman Catholic life and thought is to be found in D. S. Schaff, *Our Fathers' Faith and Ours* (G. P. Putnam's Sons, 1928) and in C. J. Cadoux, *Catholicism and Christianity* (George Allen & Unwin, London, 1928). *The Catholic Encyclopedia* is, of course, a standard reference work, and Protestants will find it helpful to consult the *Baltimore Catechism*, which has been published in many different editions.

NOTES

NOTES

Chapter I. BY WAY OF INTRODUCTION

1 George H. Tavard, *The Catholic Approach to Protestantism*, p. xiii. Harper & Brothers, 1955.
2 Elie Halévy, *A History of the English People in the Nineteenth Century*, Vol. I, p. 475. 4 vols. Peter Smith, 1949.
3 See p. 69.
4 See pp. 46, 47.
5 See pp. 51, 56.

Chapter II. THE CONSTITUTION OF THE CHURCH

1 Quoted by W. R. Inge, *Protestantism*, p. 69. Doubleday & Co., Inc., 1928.
2 *The Catholic Encyclopedia*, Vol. XII, p. 266. 15 vols. Appleton-Century-Crofts, Inc., 1907–1912.
3 Pius XII, Encyclical Letter to Chinese Catholics, *Ad Apostolorum Principis*, reprinted in the *Tablet* (Brooklyn), September 13, 1958.
4 The translation of "The First Dogmatic Constitution on the Church of Christ" is that of Cardinal Manning as printed in Geddes MacGregor, *The Vatican Revolution* (The Beacon Press, Inc., 1957), pp. 185–197. An almost identical translation is to be found in *Dogmatic Canons and Decrees* (The Devin-Adair Co., 1912); C. C. Marshall, *The Roman Catholic Church in the Modern State* (Dodd, Mead & Company, Inc., 1928; William Arthur, *The Pope,*

the Kings, and the People (Hodder & Stoughton, Ltd., London, 1903). This latter translation is apparently taken from the *Catholic Directory* for 1871.

[5] *The Pope Speaks: The Words of Pius XII*, p. 324. Harcourt, Brace and Company, Inc., 1940.

[6] *Catholic Mind*, LIII (1955), p. 319.

[7] *Current History*, XXVII (March, 1928), p. 800.

[8] *American Catholic Quarterly Review*, XIX (1894), p. 778.

[9] *Current History, loc. cit.*

[10] *American Catholic Quarterly Review*, XXVI (1901), pp. 387–388.

[11] John Wynne, ed. and tr., *The Great Encyclical Letters of Pope Leo XIII*, pp. 192–193. Benziger Brothers, Inc., 1903.

[12] *Ibid.*, p. 193.

[13] *American Catholic Quarterly Review*, XXXI (1906), pp. 213–214.

[14] *The New York Times*, August 22, 1950.

[15] Wynne, *The Great Encyclical Letters of Pope Leo XIII*, p. 189.

[16] *Ibid.*, p. 194.

[17] *Catholic Mind*, XXIX (1931), pp. 54–55.

[18] *Ibid.*, p. 55.

[19] *The New York Times*, August 22, 1950.

[20] Wynne, *The Great Encyclical Letters of Pope Leo XIII*, p. 194.

[21] *Catholic Mind*, LIII (1955), pp. 315–318.

[22] *The New York Times*, May 24, 1931.

[23] James H. Ryan, ed. and tr., *The Encyclicals of Pius XI*, pp. 40–41. B. Herder Book Company, 1927.

[24] *The New York Times*, August 22, 1950.

[25] The procedures for acquiring accurate information as to what is being taught is discussed in Appendix I, and the text of the oath required of all members of the clergy, including those serving as professors in seminaries, colleges, and universities, is also reprinted there.

[26] Vatican Press Release printed in the *American Ecclesiastical Review*, CXXXI (1954), pp. 133–134.

[27] *American Catholic Quarterly Review*, XX (1895), pp. 362–364.

CHAPTER III. THE CHRISTIAN CONSTITUTION
OF STATES

[1] Further explication of particular points of Roman Catholic
political theory are to be found in the following encyclicals of Leo XIII: "Origin of Civil Power" (*Diuturnum*),
1881; "Human Liberty" (*Libertas*), 1888; "The Chief
Duties of Christians as Citizens" (*Sapientiae christianae*), 1890; "Church and State in France" (*Au milieu
des sollicitudes*), 1892; "Catholicity in the United States"
(*Longinqua oceani*), 1895; "True and False Americanism
in Religion" (*Testem benevolentiae*), 1899; "Christian
Democracy" (*Graves de communi*), 1901.

The "fixed" principles of Roman Catholic political doctrine were summarized by Pius X in the *Condemnation
of the* Sillon, August 25, 1910. Additional elaboration of
certain features of Roman Catholic political theory is to
be found in the encyclicals of Piux X, *E Supremi* (1903)
and *Vehementer Nos* (1906); of Pius XI, *Ubi arcano*
(1922) and *Quas primas* (1925); and of Pius XII, *Summi
Pontificatus* (1939). Of these latter documents, *Quas primas* provides the most complete statement of the doctrinal basis of Roman Catholic political theory. Pius XII
points out that in this encyclical Pius XI "laid down the
official teaching about the authority of Jesus Christ our
King and that of His Church" (*The Pope Speaks: The
Words of Pius XII,* p. 187).

[2] *Catholic Mind,* XXXIV (1936), pp. 425–449.
[3] Ryan, *Encyclicals of Pius XI,* pp. 140–141.
[4] *Ibid.,* pp. 153–154.
[5] *Tablet* (London), (July 16, 1881), p. 110.
[6] *Ibid.,* p. 109.
[7] *Ibid.*
[8] *Catholic World,* XXVIII (1878–1879), pp. 853–854.
[9] *American Catholic Quarterly Review,* XXXV (1910), pp.
693–696.
[10] *Ibid.,* p. 697.
[11] *Ibid.,* pp. 699–700.
[12] *Ibid.,* pp. 702–703.

[13] *American Catholic Quarterly Review,* XXXV, pp. 705–707.
[14] *Tablet* (London), July 14, 1888, p. 46.
[15] Wynne, *The Great Encyclical Letters of Pope Leo XIII,* pp. 183–184.
[16] *Ibid.,* p. 185.
[17] Ryan, *Encyclicals of Pius XI,* p. 23.
[18] *Ibid.,* p. 30.
[19] *American Catholic Quarterly Review,* XXXI (1906), p. 211.
[20] *The Pope Speaks: The Words of Pius XII,* p. 174.
[21] *Tablet* (London), July 14, 1888, p. 44.
[22] *Ibid.*
[23] *Ibid.,* p. 45.
[24] Wynne, *The Great Encyclical Letters of Pope Leo XIII,* p. 158.
[25] *American Catholic Quarterly Review,* XXIV (1899), April, pp. 193–194.
[26] *Ibid.,* XX (1895), pp. 357–360, 365.

CHAPTER IV. CHRISTIAN DEMOCRACY

[1] F. J. Powers, *Papal Pronouncements on the Political Order,* p. 48. The Newman Press, 1952.
[2] *Tablet* (London), July 14, 1888, p. 46.
[3] See pp. 64, 73, 83, 102–105.
[4] Eduardo Soderini, *The Pontificate of Leo XIII,* tr. B. B. Carter, p. 208. Burns, Oates & Washbourne, London, 1934.
[5] *American Catholic Quarterly Review,* XXVI (1901), pp. 385–386.
[6] *Ibid.,* XXVIII (1903), p. 388.
[7] *The New York Times,* December 25, 1944.

CHAPTER V. CATHOLIC ACTION

[1] See p. 136.
[2] See pp. 140–141. *American Catholic Quarterly Review,* XXIX (1904), p. 234. See also Luigi Civardi, *A Manual of Catholic Action,* p. 26 n. Sheed & Ward, Inc., 1936.
[3] *American Catholic Quarterly Review,* XXIX (1904), pp. 234–239.

[4] Civardi, *op. cit.*, pp. 4–6.
[5] *Ibid.*, p. 54.
[6] *Ibid.*, p. 198.
[7] *Catholic Mind*, XLIX (1951), pp. 524–527.
[8] *Ibid.*, L (1952), pp. 115–121.
[9] *Ibid.*, LVI (1958), pp. 75–90.
[10] *American Catholic Quarterly Review*, XXIX (1904), pp. 11, 14, 17–18.
[11] *Ibid.*, XX (1895), pp. 865–866.
[12] *Ibid.*, XXVI (1901), pp. 392–394.
[13] Vatican Press Release printed in the *American Ecclesiastical Review*, CXXXI (1954), pp. 133–134.
[14] *Ibid.*, p. 136.
[15] *American Catholic Quarterly Review*, XXVI (1901), p. 392.
[16] *American Ecclesiastical Review*, CXXXI (1954), p. 136.
[17] *American Catholic Quarterly Review*, XXXV (1910), p. 695.
[18] *Catholic Mind*, XLV (1947), p. 454.
[19] *Ibid.*, XLVIII (1950), p. 60.
[20] *Ibid.*, XLVI (1948), p. 76.
[21] *Ibid.*, XLVIII (1950), p. 190.
[22] *American Catholic Quarterly Review*, XX (1895), pp. 366–367.

CHAPTER VI. CONCLUDING OBSERVATIONS

[1] See p. 52. *Catholic Mind*, LIII (1955), p. 315.
[2] This summary is taken from James H. Nichols, *Democracy and the Churches* (The Westminster Press, 1951), pp. 102–103. The authorities on which it is based are: Liguori, *Praxis confessarii*, Capit. primum, § II, circa medici officium, 8, 9; Koch-Preuss, *Handbook of Moral Theology* (B. Herder Book Company, 1919–1925), II, pp. 164, 165; and McHugh and Callan, *Moral Theology* (Joseph F. Wagner, Inc., 1929–1930), II, p. 703.
[3] See pp. 67–68, 118.
[4] See pp. 71–73, 78–79, 80, 97–98.
[5] *Two Basic Social Encyclicals*, pp. 23–27, 141–151. Benziger Brothers, Inc., 1943.

⁶ Pius XI, Encyclical on Christian Marriage, *Catholic Mind,* XXIX (1931), pp. 29, 44.
⁷ *The New York Times,* February 21, 1946.
⁸ See p. 50.
⁹ *America: The National Catholic Weekly,* February 18, 1950. *The Catholic Encyclopedia,* Vol. XIV, pp. 763–773.
¹⁰ "Freedom of Religion," *Theological Studies,* March, 1945, p. 96.
¹¹ This summary of Father Murray's views on this specific topic has been drawn from his article "Freedom of Religion," pp. 85–113, *Theological Studies,* March, 1945. See also his article "Freedom of Religion," pp. 229–286, *Theological Studies,* June, 1945. The main features of his position, the status of which even as a permissible point of view within the Roman Church is highly problematical, have been elaborated in numerous articles — the more important of which are: "The Problem of 'The Religion of the State,'" *American Ecclesiastical Review,* May, 1951; "For the Freedom and Transcendence of the Church," *ibid.,* January, 1952; "Catholics in America," *Catholic Mind,* October, 1955; "St. Robert Bellarmine on the Indirect Power," *Theological Studies,* December, 1948; "Contemporary Orientations of Catholic Thought on Church and State in the Light of History," *ibid.,* June, 1949; "Current Theology on Religious Freedom," *ibid.,* September, 1949; "The Church and Totalitarian Democracy," *ibid.,* December, 1952; "Leo XIII: Separation of Church and State," *ibid.,* June, 1953; "Leo XIII: Two Concepts of Government," *ibid.,* December, 1953; "The Problem of Pluralism in America," *Thought,* Summer, 1954; "On the Structure of the Church-State Problem," in Waldemar Gurian and M. A. Fitzsimmons, *The Catholic Church in World Affairs* (University of Notre Dame, 1954).

Numerous articles in the *American Ecclesiastical Review,* published by Catholic University, have contended that Murray's views fall clearly within the scope of successive papal condemnations: F. J. Connell, "The Theory of the Lay State," July, 1951, and a "Reply to Father

Murray," January, 1952; J. C. Fenton, "The Status of a Controversy," June, 1951, "The Teaching of *Testem benevolentiae*," August, 1953, "Toleration and the Church-State Controversy," May, 1954, "Catholic Polemic and Doctrinal Accuracy," February, 1955; Alfred Cardinal Ottaviani, "Church and State: Some Present Problems in the Light of the Teaching of Pope Pius XII," May, 1953; and G. W. Shea, "Catholic Doctrine and 'The Religion of the State,'" September, 1950, and "Catholic Orientations in Church and State," December, 1951.

[12] *The Commonweal*, May 30, 1958, p. 229.

[13] *American Ecclesiastical Review*, CXXXI (1954), pp. 132–137. For a discussion of the significance of this allocution, see *ibid.*, pp. 186–198. A continuation of this allocution was delivered at a later date; see "The Teaching Authority of the Church," *Catholic Mind*, LIII (1955), pp. 311–320.

APPENDIX A. THE CONSOLIDATION OF PAPAL CONTROL UNDER PIUS X

[1] *American Catholic Quarterly Review*, XXIX (1904), pp. 10–19.

[2] *Ibid.*, XXXIII (1908), pp. 505–516.

[3] *Ibid.*, XXIX (1904), pp. 234–239.

[4] *Ibid.*, XXIX (1904), pp. 588–603; XXI (1906), pp. 744–750; XXXIII (1908), pp. 517–553; XXXIV (1909), pp. 547–569; XXXV (1910), pp. 384–412.

[5] *Ibid.*, XXIX (1904), p. 550.

[6] *Ibid.*, XXXII (1907), pp. 561–566, 705–730.

[7] *Ibid.*, XXXIII (1908), p. 155.

[8] *Ibid.*, XXXV (1910), pp. 712–731.

[9] *Ibid.*, pp. 723–724.

APPENDIX B. ESSENTIAL CHARACTERISTICS OF EX CATHEDRA PRONOUNCEMENTS

[1] M. C. Carlen, *A Guide to the Encyclicals of the Roman Pontiffs*, p. 8. The H. W. Wilson Company, 1939.

INDEX

INDEX

Antimodernist oath, 169–172
"Apostolate of the Laity, The," 134–140
Apostolic Delegate, role of, in U.S., 59–61
Apostolic succession, 34, 37

Bible, 18–21, 56
Biblical Commission, 167 f.
Bill of Rights, 156, 160
Bossuet, Bishop, 28

Canossa, 26
Catholic Action, 12, 63, 86–89, 122–147, 152; definition of, 122, 125, 136 f.; goal of, 65, 88, 123 f., 125 f., 140 f., 165 f.; origin of, 122–124, 130 f., 136; scope of, 128, 131, 134, 136, 138–140, 145–147; subordination to hierarchy, 65, 88, 124 f., 127 f., 129, 132 f., 142, 147
"Catholic Action," 126–129
Cavour, 62
Censorship, 58 f., 167–169

Charlemagne, 25
Christ the King, Feast of, 90 f.
"Christian Constitution of States, The": discussed, 62–66; text, 66–90
Christmas Message of 1944: discussed, 108–112; text, 114–121
Church and state, 63 f., 69–73, 81–83, 97–105, 151; mixed jurisdiction, 53, 55, 71–73, 78, 83, 97 f., 99, 151
Clement XIV, 29
Commonweal, The, 159
Conciliarism, 19 f., 26 f., 28, 32, 42
Conscience, freedom of, 154. *See also* Religious freedom
Constance, Council of, 27
Constitution of the church, the: discussed, 31–37; text, 37–45
Curia, 166

Democracy: adjustment to, 73, 83, 102–104, 106 f., 155–

Restoration of 1814, 29
Roman Catholic liberalism, 22–24, 155–160
Roman Catholicism: Constitution of the church, the, 30–45; distinctive and essential character, 31, 48, 159–161, 169; modern character of, 24–30, 165; relationship to state, 63 f., 69–73, 81–83, 97–105; teaching authority, 16 f., 18–22, 48–59, 99, 142 f., 144, 159 f.; utopian character of, 21, 150 f.
Roman obedience, 24, 31, 150, 154, 161

Schism of 1378–1417, 26 f.
Si diligis, 58 f., 142 f., 144, 160, 172, 185
Sillon, 93–97, 144 f.

Tavard, George H., 15
"Teaching Authority of the Church, The," 45 f., 52–55
Theologians, authority of, 16, 22–24, 50–52, 56–58
Thomism, 167
Trent, Council of, 19, 27 f.

Ultramontanism, 24, 28–30, 165–172
United States: not a model, 104–105; role of Apostolic Delegate, 59–61
Utopianism, 21, 150 f.

Vatican Council, 20, 30 f., 37
Vocation, Protestant doctrine of, 152–154

William the Conqueror, 25 f.
Worker-Priests of France, 153, 160

Date Due

25 '60	MAR 25 '87		
May 3			
MAY 13 '60			
APR 28 '61			
MAY 23 '61			
MAR 23 '62			
APR 17 '64			
APR 20 '66			
OCT 18 '66			
DEC 1 '68			
OCT 28 '68			
April 1 MAY 8 '69			
MAY 20 '69			
'69			
DEC 21 '84			